AF702492

Presented to you by:

Vetter Health Services

"Dignity In Life"

www.VetterHealthServices.com

NEBRASKA

CENTERED ON THE LAND

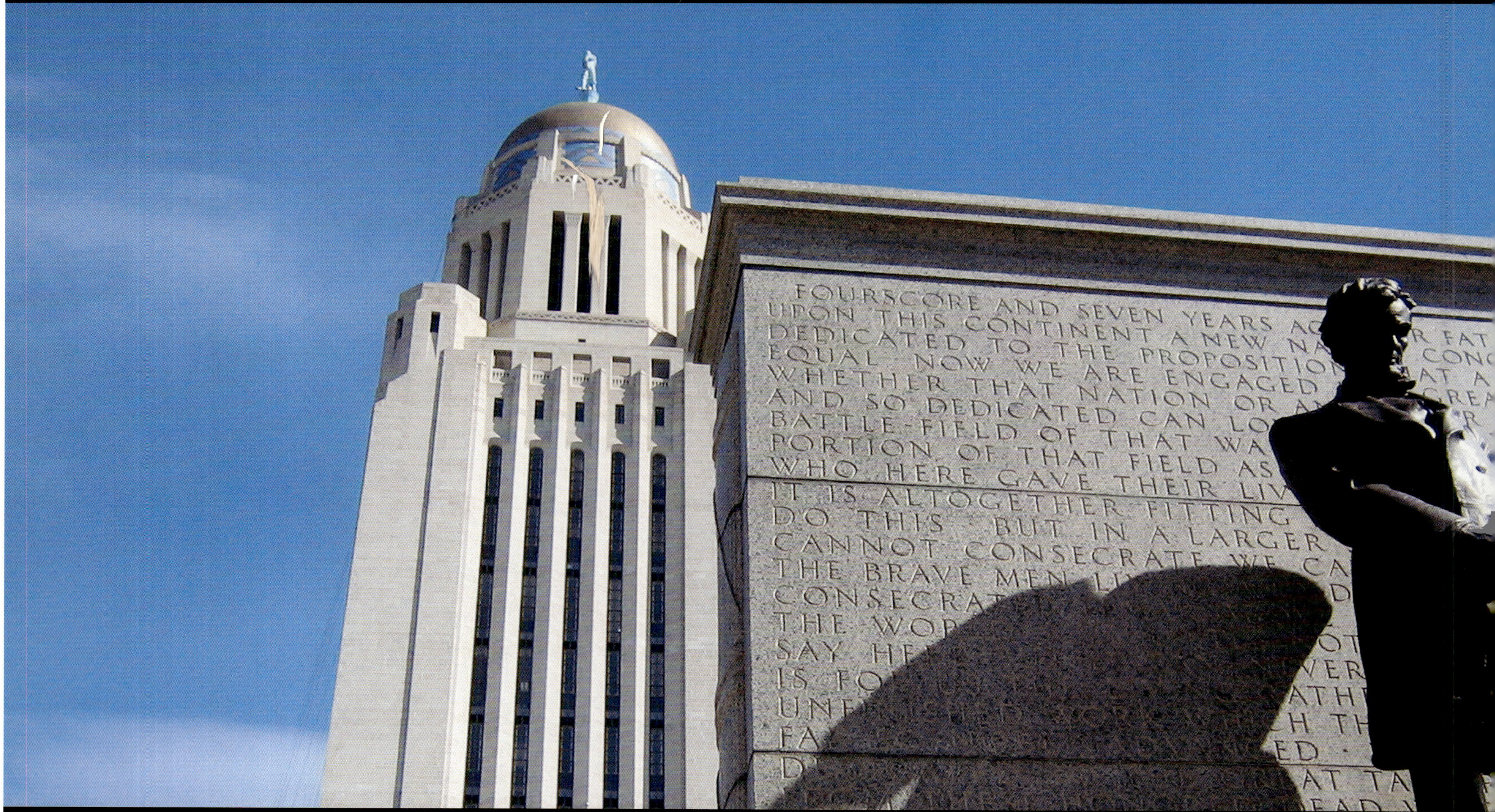

Nebraska state capitol, Lincoln

NEBRASKA

CENTERED ON THE LAND

CINDY MURPHY McMAHON and MICHAEL GOODWIN

This book was produced in cooperation with the Nebraska Department of Economic Development. Cherbo Publishing Group gratefully acknowledges its important contribution to *Nebraska: Centered on the Land*.

cherbo publishing group, inc.

president	JACK C. CHERBO
executive vice president	ELAINE HOFFMAN
editorial director	CHRISTINA M. BEAUSANG
managing feature editor	MARGARET L. MARTIN
feature editor	B. D. CAMPBELL
senior profiles editor	J. KELLEY YOUNGER
profiles editors	BENJAMIN PROST
	LIZA YETENEKIAN SMITH
associate editor	SYLVIA EMRICH-TOMA
proofreaders	ELIZABETH FENNER
	JENNY KORNFELD
profiles writers	DIANE V. ANDERSON
	LINDA CHASE
	SYLVIA EMRICH-TOMA
	KATHLEEN GILBERT
	TERRI JONISCH
	TERRAN LAMP
	RODD MONTS
	STEFANIE SPIKELL
	BILL STEIN
creative director	PERI A. HOLGUIN
senior designer	THEODORE E. YEAGER
profiles designer	NELSON CAMPOS
photo editors	WALTER MLADINA
	DAVID ZANZINGER
digital color specialist	ART VASQUEZ
sales administrator	JOAN K. BAKER
profile services supervisor	PATRICIA DE LEONARD
profile services coordinators	KENYA HICKS
	LESLIE E. SHAW
administrative assistants	JUDY ROBITSCHEK
	BILL WAY
southwest regional manager	JOHN T. HECKER
publisher's representative	BOB FREEMAN

Cherbo Publishing Group, Inc.
Encino, California 91316
© 2007 by Cherbo Publishing Group, Inc.
All rights reserved.
Published 2006

Printed in Canada
By Friesens

Subsidiary Production Office
Santa Rosa, CA, USA
888.340.6049

Library of Congress Cataloging-in-Publication data
McMahon, Cindy Murphy and Michael Goodwin.
A pictorial guide highlighting Nebraska's economic and social advantages.
Library of Congress Control Number: 2006932536
ISBN 978-1-882933-75-4

Visit the CPG Web site at www.cherbopub.com.

The information in this publication is the most recent available, has been carefully researched to ensure accuracy, and has been reviewed by the sponsor. Cherbo Publishing Group, Inc., cannot and does not guarantee either the correctness of all information furnished it or the complete absence of errors, including omissions.

Dedication and Acknowledgments

Cindy Murphy McMahon dedicates her portion of this book to her husband, Tom; her parents, Bob and Norma Murphy; and her sons, Matt, Dan, and Mike. She would like to thank all those who gave of their time and talents to help her tell the story of life in Nebraska. She especially wishes to thank Pulitzer Prize winner Ted Kooser, U.S. Poet Laureate from 2004 to 2006, for granting her permission to quote "A Winter Morning" from his book *Delights & Shadows* (Port Townsend, WA: Copper Canyon Press, 2004). Kooser single-handedly has boosted Nebraskans' pride to an even higher level.

Michael Goodwin dedicates his portion of this book to his family, who support him in all that he does. Many people helped him complete this project. One who deserves special recognition is B. D. Campbell, his editor at Cherbo Publishing Group, whose insights and suggestions he found invaluable while writing and revising the text. His patience and encouragement were also much appreciated. As well, a number of industry professionals and information officers graciously provided Goodwin with data and pointed him toward good sources. Most important of all, however, was his wife, Megan, who always encourages him.

Left to right: Holy Family Shrine, Omaha skyline, capitol rotunda

TABLE OF CONTENTS

Left to right: Windmills, Henry Doorly Zoo, Holmes Lake near Lincoln

COMPANIES & ORGANIZATIONS PROFILED

The following organizations have made a valuable commitment to the quality of this publication. The Nebraska Department of Economic Development gratefully acknowledges their participation in *Nebraska: Centered on the Land.*

Berkshire Hathaway stockholders meeting

BUSINESS VISIONARIES

The following companies and organizations are recognized as innovators in their fields and have played a prominent role in this publication, as they have in the state.

Alegent Health
2001 South 75th Street, Omaha, NE 68124
Contact: Dina Maas, Public Relations Specialist
Phone: 402-398-5653 / Fax: 402-398-6032
E-mail: dmaas@alegent.org
Web site: www.alegent.com

Eaton Corporation
Hastings Plant
300 East 39th Street, Hastings, NE 68901

Kearney Plant
4200 Highway 30 East, Kearney, NE 68847

Corporate Headquarters
Eaton Center, 1111 Superior Avenue, Cleveland, OH 44114

Web site: www.eaton.com

Behlen Mfg. Co.
4025 East 23rd Street, Columbus, NE 68601
Contact: Phil Raimondo, President
Phone: 402-564-3111 / Fax: 402-563-7405
E-mail: behlen@behlenmfg.com
Web site: www.behlenmfg.com
"Where Teamwork and Change Make Customers and Employees Better Off"

FirstComp Insurance
Central Park Plaza South
222 South 15th Street, Suite 1200, Omaha, NE 68102
Contact: Andy Williams, Communications Manager
Phone: 888-500-3344 / Fax: 866-338-2667
E-mail: awilliams@firstcomp.com
Web site: www.firstcomp.com
"Insuring America's Small Business"

Creighton University
2500 California Plaza, Omaha, NE 68178
Contact: Don Bishop, Associate Vice President, Enrollment Management
Phone: 402-280-2700
E-mail: admissions@creighton.edu
Web site: www.creighton.edu

Continued on page xiv

BUSINESS VISIONARIES

The following companies and organizations are recognized as innovators in their fields and have played a prominent role in this publication, as they have in the state.

Continued from page xii

First National Bank
1620 Dodge Street, Omaha, NE 68197
Phone: 800-228-4411 / Fax: 402-633-2220
Web site: www.firstnational.com

State Farm Insurance Companies
222 South 84th Street, Lincoln, NE 68510
Contact: Shane Herrera, Human Resources Manager
Phone: 402-327-3299 / Fax: 402-327-5303
E-mail: shaneherrera.c0lc@statefarm.com
Web site: www.statefarm.com
"Like a good neighbor, State Farm is there.®"

Noddle Companies
1125 South 103rd Street, Suite 450, Omaha, NE 68124
Phone: 402-496-1616 / Fax: 402-496-6250
Web site: www.noddlecompanies.com

Vetter Health Services, Inc.
5020 South 118th Street, Omaha, NE 68137
Phone: 402-895-3932 / Fax: 402-895-8165
Contact: Jack Vetter, Founder/President
E-mail: jvetter@vhsmail.com
Web site: www.vetterhealthservices.com
"Dignity In Life"

Omaha Public Power District
444 South 16th Street Mall, Omaha, NE 68102
Contact: W. Gary Gates, President and CEO
Phone: 402-636-2000 / Fax: 402-636-3922
E-mail: webmaster@oppd.com
Web site: www.oppd.com
"Your Energy Partner"

Left to right: Living history at Great Platte River Road Archway Monument, July Jamm in Lincoln, Nebraskaland Days in North Platte

Left to right: Soybean fields, Arbor Day, botany class at UN Kearney

FOREWORD

Nebraska is alive with opportunities for families and businesses. With our wonderfully diverse cultural heritage and our strong midwestern work ethic, there's no better place to build, expand, or start a business, and there's no better place to live.

My vision for Nebraska is based on four priorities: education, economic vitality, efficiency in government, and protecting families.

Nebraska offers an endless array of advantages that make living, playing, working, and doing business here a wonderful and rewarding experience. We have one of the best quality-of-life ratings in America, an overall cost of living that is less than the national average, an outstanding educational system, a great work ethic, some of the nation's shortest commuting times, a strong and healthy economy, and a business-friendly atmosphere. Within our borders you'll discover people who are genuine, hardworking, and proud of their heritage. Nebraskans are excited about the future and eagerly welcome new people, industry, and development to the state.

Many companies in the United States and around the world have discovered that Nebraska offers the ideal location, quality workforce, and positive economic environment for a wide variety of industries and business endeavors.

As you explore the pages of this book, think of the vast opportunities that await you in Nebraska. People who come to Nebraska are often amazed by what they find. We are a destination, and as a native Nebraskan, I've never given any thought to living anywhere but right here in Nebraska.

Dave Heineman

Dave Heineman
Governor, State of Nebraska

GOVERNOR'S SEAL · STATE OF NEBRASKA

NEBRASKA TIMELINE

1806 Zebulon Pike explores southern Nebraska.

1682 Explorer and fur trader Sieur LaSalle claims all lands drained by the Mississippi and its tributaries for France.

1682

1720 Pedro de Villasur leads a group of Spanish soldiers into Nebraska to reclaim the plains from the French. The Pawnee Indians kill most members of the expedition near what is now Columbus, Nebraska.

1739 French explorers Pierre and Paul Mallet travel across the length of Nebraska looking for a route to Santa Fe.

1763 Spain gains control of all lands west of the Mississippi following the French and Indian War.

1800 Spain cedes the Louisiana territory to France.

1803 The United States acquires eastern Nebraska from France through the Louisiana Purchase.

1822

1804 Lewis and Clark explore the eastern edge of Nebraska.

1813 Robert Stuart establishes the Oregon Trail, part of which travels through Nebraska's Platte Valley.

1819 The U.S. Army establishes Fort Atkinson, Nebraska's first military post.

1822 Oglala Lakota leader Red Cloud is born near modern-day North Platte.

1714 French explorer Etienne Veniard de Bourgmont becomes the first recorded European to explore Nebraska.

1860 Pony Express establishes stations throughout the Platte River Valley.

1823 1869

1823 Fur trader Manuel Lisa establishes Bellevue, the first white settlement in Nebraska.

1830 Jedediah Smith travels west along what will become the Oregon Trail.

1842 John C. Frémont explores the Platte Valley and calls the area "Nebraska," an Oto Indian word for "flat water."

1848 The United States acquires western Nebraska following the Mexican War.

1854 Congress passes the Kansas-Nebraska Act, which designates Nebraska as a U.S. territory. The territory's white population grows from 2,732 in November of 1854 to over 28,000 in 1860.

1854 The *Nebraska Palladium*, the Nebraska Territory's first newspaper, is founded.

1862 The Homestead Act gives settlers free land in exchange for living on and developing the land. Eastern Nebraska's white population increases from 29,000 to 123,000 in just 10 years.

1867 Nebraska becomes the 37th state.

1868 Lincoln replaces Omaha as the state capital.

1869 Red Cloud and other Sioux leaders sign the Treaty of Fort Laramie. The Sioux nation's land extends south of the Platte River.

1883 William “Buffalo Bill” Cody stages the first theatrical Wild West show in North Platte. The show will later feature sharpshooter Annie Oakley and perform in New York City and throughout Europe.

1872

1872 J. Sterling Morton, of Nebraska City, establishes Arbor Day. It is claimed that a million trees were planted on its first observance.

1877 Oglala leader Crazy Horse surrenders at Camp Robinson.

1891 The Federal Division of Forestry begins planting trees in Holt County. These pine reserves become the Nebraska National Forest in 1908.

1895 Silas Robbins becomes the first African-American admitted to the Nebraska State Bar Association.

1934 The *Pioneer Zephyr*, the first streamlined, stainless-steel, diesel-powered train, begins its regular route between Kansas City, Missouri, and Omaha and Lincoln, Nebraska.

1898

1938

1898 Omaha hosts the first National Log Rolling Championship, an event that remains popular to this day.

1902 The Reclamation Act of 1902 earmarks federal aid for irrigation projects.

1922 University of Nebraska–Lincoln alumna and novelist Willa Cather wins a Pulitzer Prize for *One of Ours*.

1927 The University of Nebraska–Lincoln's *The Prairie Schooner*, one of the nation's oldest literary magazines, begins publication.

1927 Edwin E. Perkins of Hastings invents Kool-Aid.

1937 Nebraska creates the nation's first unicameral legislature.

1938 Mildred Brown, the first African-American to be inducted into the Omaha Business Hall of Fame, founds the *Omaha Star*, a newspaper that reports local and national news from an African-American perspective.

1917 Father Edward Flanagan establishes Boys Town.

1920 Civil rights leader Malcom X is born in Omaha.

1940 The U.S. government commissions the building of the Martin Bomber Plant in Bellevue, which would produce over 1,500 B-26 Marauder medium bombers and 500 B-29 Superfortresses for use in World War II.

1940

1954

1943 Warren Buffett, the Oracle of Omaha, age 13, files his first income tax return.

1945 Nebraska's state nickname is changed from the Tree Planters' State to the Cornhusker State.

1948 Frank Zybach invents the center-pivot irrigation machine, revolutionizing irrigation technology. Nebraska later becomes the largest producer and user of center-pivot irrigation systems.

1948 Strategic Air Command (SAC) moves to Offut Air Force Base.

1950 Omaha becomes the home of the College World Series.

1954 Omaha native Marlon Brando wins the Academy Award for Best Actor for his performance in *On the Waterfront.*

1958 University of Nebraska–Lincoln alumnus George Beadle receives a Nobel Prize for his work in biochemistry.

1965 The Buffalo Bill Ranch in North Platte becomes a state historical park.

1958

1963 Demonstrations for the civil rights of African-Americans lead to the establishment of the Omaha Human Rights Commission.

1972 Omaha becomes one of the first cities to use glasphalt, a mixture of asphalt and recycled glass, to pave roads.

1962 Norfolk native Johnny Carson takes over as host of *The Tonight Show.*

1986 Nebraska native Kay A. Orr becomes the first female Republican governor in U.S. history.

1974

1977 Chicago Bears football player Gale Sayers, raised in Omaha, enters the Pro Football Hall of Fame.

1982 Nebraska's constitution is amended to prevent rangeland and farmland from being sold to nonfamily corporations.

1987 To encourage job growth, the Nebraska Legislature adopts two measures authorizing tax incentives.

1981 Bob Gibson, Omaha native and pitcher for the St. Louis Cardinals for over 15 years, is elected to the Baseball Hall of Fame.

1974 Gerald Ford of Omaha becomes the 38th president of the United States.

1987 University of Nebraska–Lincoln alumnus Donald Cram shares the Nobel Prize in chemistry.

2006 Shelby native Curt Tomasevicz competes in the four-man bobsled race in the Winter Olympic Games in Turin, Italy.

1987

1991 A copy of Shakespeare's First Folio, published in 1623, is added to the collection at the Don L. Love Memorial Library at the University of Nebraska–Lincoln.

1992 SAC becomes U.S. Strategic Command (USSTRATCOM).

1999 Tom Osborne, head football coach for the Nebraska Cornhuskers for over 20 years, is inducted into the College Football Hall of Fame.

2001 Dick Cheney, born in Lincoln, becomes the 46th vice president of the United States under President George W. Bush.

2006

2004 Ted Kooser, alumnus and professor in the English department at the University of Nebraska–Lincoln, is appointed U.S. poet laureate. He is the first poet laureate chosen from the Great Plains.

2005 Nebraska Advantage business incentives package makes its debut.

2003 Professional tennis player Andy Roddick, an Omaha native, wins his first Grand Slam title at the U.S. Open.

Sand Hills Golf Club

PART ONE
THE GOOD LIFE: AN OVERVIEW OF NEBRASKA

BY CINDY MURPHY McMAHON

THERE IS NO PLACE LIKE NEBRASKA:
Quality of Life

Entertainments in Nebraska range from the down-home wholesomeness of "Nebraska's Big Rodeo" in Burwell (opposite page) to the urban sophistication of grand opera and Broadway productions at the Orpheum Theater (this page) in Omaha.

A farmhouse window far back from the highway

Speaks to the darkness in a small, sure voice.

Against this stillness, only a kettle's whisper,

And against the starry cold, one small blue ring of flame.

—Ted Kooser, "A Winter Morning"

Such pure, eloquent language captivates the hearts and minds of those who read the verse of Nebraska's Ted Kooser, U.S. poet laureate and Pulitzer Prize winner, but hard facts and figures have something to say about Nebraska, too. Just a few of the state's boasts: a consistently low unemployment rate, a commercially advantageous central location between both coasts, four full seasons, and—just for fun—the number-one golf course in the country. Morgan Quitno Press rates Nebraska among its top 10 most-livable states, and the American Automobile Association rates it as the country's most economical travel destination.

Much of Nebraska is flat, it's true. Its name comes from the Oto Indian word *nebrathka*, which means "flat water" and is presumed by historians to refer to the Platte River. But "flat" doesn't begin to describe multifarious Nebraska. There's nothing plain about this Great Plains state, from the rugged charisma of its western panhandle to the wide panoramas of its central agricultural regions to the educational, business, and health care meccas of its urbanized eastern edge.

Once a welcome landmark to westward-bound settlers, Chimney Rock (above right) now serves as its own historic monument. Carhenge (below right), north of Alliance in the Sand Hills region, serves as a whimsical monument to today's air-conditioned pioneers who cruise along the state's east-west artery, Interstate 80 (below).

The land itself—which straddles two time zones, covers 77,358 square miles, and is home to 1.7 million people—is as varied today as it was when the pioneers crossed it via the Oregon and Mormon trails. When the members of the Lewis and Clark expedition set foot in the state in 1804, they marveled at the land's openness and diversity; today's explorers find that although Interstate 80 makes it easy to cross the state's nearly 500-mile expanse, much can be experienced by veering off the superhighway's straight path. State tourism officials have mapped out nine back-road excursions, called Nebraska's Scenic Byways, that display some of the state's most striking historical and natural features.

Nebraska can be conveniently divided into seven distinct districts. The Panhandle, the formidable westernmost region, challenged pioneers and cattle drivers with its rocky canyons and stately pine forests. Three of the sights—two of them natural and one man-made—that intrigue today's travelers are grazing herds of bison, towering Chimney Rock, and Carhenge, Nebraska's tongue-in-cheek answer to England's Stonehenge.

Just east of the Panhandle, the Sand Hills is the largest region—an inspirational 19,000 square miles of authentic prairie. There may be no other place on Earth that features mound upon mound of grass-covered sand dunes interspersed with clear, swift rivers that are popular with canoeists. And there's definitely nowhere else that can claim a completely man-made national forest.

Opposite page: Sandhill cranes fly over the Platte River Valley near Kearny during their annual migration. Center: The Platte River, said to be "a mile wide and an inch deep," traverses the length of the state from west to east. This page: A kayaker explores the Niobrara National Scenic River in the Sand Hills.

Sparkling lakes and reservoirs dot the Prairie Lakes area in the southwestern part of the state—a veritable fishing and boating paradise. Nebraska ranks second only to Minnesota for the number of lakes it holds. But historically, it was William F. "Buffalo Bill" Cody who drew attention here with his Wild West Show, which Nebraskans claim as the first organized rodeo and memorialize to this day. The region is also home to the world's largest classification yard (where rail cars are grouped into trains according to destination), a fact not wasted on train enthusiasts.

Wetlands and marshes give the Frontier Trails area in south-central Nebraska its personality. Delighted birders come from all over each spring to witness a half-million sandhill cranes gather in the Platte River Valley. The area was inspiration to Pulitzer Prize–winning author Willa Cather.

Rolling hills that give way to the leafy banks of the Missouri River characterize Pioneer Country in southeastern Nebraska. Abundant and fascinating wildlife make this area a favorite of both animal watchers and hunters. It includes lush, well-treed Nebraska City, home to Arbor Day and many related attractions.

The plains and hills take a back seat to tall buildings and hundreds of thousands of humans in the population centers of Omaha and Lincoln, which make up the Metropolitan area. The urban hubs feature state government, universities, award-winning medical centers, arts and entertainment, and dining and shopping. And that's not to mention some of the state's top tourist draws, including a world-famous zoo.

Below: An afternoon sky lights up Omaha's office towers.
Opposite: A storm adds drama to corn and cattle country near North Platte.

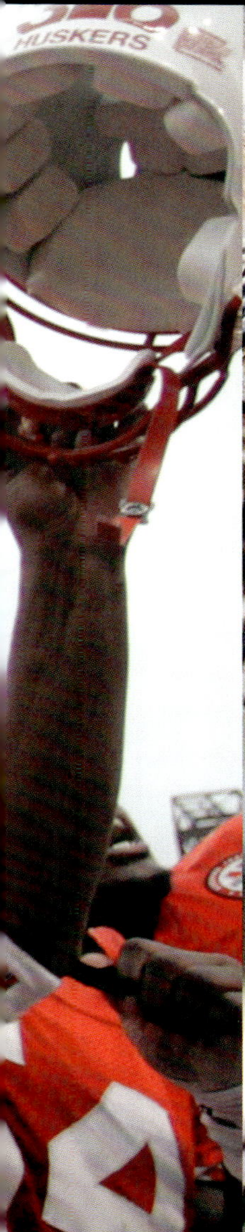

Opposite page, left to right: Cornhuskers Daniel Bullocks, Wali Muhammad, and Cory Ross celebrate a victory over the Iowa State Cyclones in Lincoln. This page: Nebraska's Native American tribes include the Missouri, Omaha, Ponca, Pawnee, and Cheyenne peoples, 15,000 of whom currently live in the state.

Named for the famed explorers, the northeastern Lewis and Clark region is the state's center of American Indian culture. Visitors here can encounter fossils that are millions of years old, enjoy beautiful state parks, learn about Native Americans, and view the wild Missouri River as Lewis and Clark did before dams tamed its flow.

The People

The University of Nebraska's football team, the Cornhuskers, is a great unifying force in Nebraska. Rural and urban dwellers alike follow the fate—good or bad—of the five-time national champions. But long before the Cornhuskers were tossing footballs, or the farmers for whom the team is named were husking corn, people hunted and farmed here. About a dozen American Indian tribes, including the Missouri, Omaha, Ponca, Pawnee, and Cheyenne, called Nebraska home. Some 15,000 Native Americans live here, and the state is home to three reservations. Many attractions throughout the state teach visitors about American Indian culture and customs.

When Napoleon Bonaparte sold Louisiana—a vast territory that included eastern Nebraska—to the United States in 1803, President Thomas Jefferson was eager to see what he had bought. He dispatched explorers Meriwether Lewis and William Clark, who traveled along the state's eastern border; traders and settlers soon followed. The city of Bellevue, Nebraska's oldest, began life as a

This page: Patrons enjoy an afternoon concert at the Joslyn Art Museum in Omaha. Opposite page, top: Dancers make merry at the Czech Festival in Wilber. Opposite page, bottom: The Paul Taylor Dance Company performs at the refurbished Orpheum Theater in Omaha.

trading post in the 1820s. In 1854, the Kansas-Nebraska Act made the territory official, and Nebraska became the 37th state of the Union in 1867. Farms, ranches, railroads, and meatpacking plants brought jobs and growth. German, Irish, English, Czech, and Scandinavian immigrants, among others, eased into Nebraska and began raising families.

Nebraskans have always been an independent and practical bunch. Maybe that's why the state has the nation's only unicameral (one house) legislature, created by the voters in 1934. The senators in the Legislature are also officially nonpartisan, which keeps political party rhetoric at a lower pitch than in many other places. Nebraska has three U.S. congressional districts and five electoral votes.

People who live in Nebraska tend to take their various faiths seriously. A 2006 Gallup poll found that Nebraskans are among the most frequent worshippers in the nation, with 53 percent reporting they attend a place of worship regularly.

Community Life

Today, Nebraska is home to 530 incorporated towns or cities, ranging in size from tiny Brewster, population 22, to the Omaha metropolitan area, with a population hovering around 813,000. Many communities have retained their ethnic roots, such as Wilber, home of the Czech Festival; Dannebrog, the "Danish Capital of Nebraska"; and O'Neill, the state's "Irish Capital."

Omaha proper, once a rough-hewn town with railroad and stockyard roots, has grown up to be a burgeoning metropolis of more than 414,000 people. Named one of *Money* magazine's 10 Best Big Cities in 2006, it exhibits steady economic growth and low unemployment. Riverfront development and urban renewal are the order of the day, and the third-lowest commute time among

cities over 250,000 is a major bragging point. Young people are also quite proud that Omaha is considered an "indie" music capital.

Lincoln, the seat of state government, sports a 400-foot-tall capitol building that can be seen from afar and is popular with tourists. Known as the Prairie Capital City and with a population of about 236,000, Lincoln is home to the University of Nebraska's largest campus. It claims numerous high rankings for a variety of "best cities" categories, including having more park acres per capita than any other city in the United States.

Bellevue, which has a population approaching 50,000, lies on Omaha's southern outskirts and is adjacent to Offutt Air Force Base. Offutt, the home of U.S. Strategic Command (USSTRATCOM), is a central bastion in the nation's post–September 11th defenses.

More centrally located than Nebraska's other main cities, Grand Island is officially the state's fourth largest, with a population of 44,000. Visitors especially enjoy the living-history Stuhr Museum of the Prairie Pioneer. Grand Island celebrates its German roots, but has broadened its festivities to include the many ethnic groups that now make up the community with the annual Central Nebraska Ethnic Festival.

Enjoying Life

In a state as divergent as Nebraska, it naturally follows that there is an abundance of ways to have fun, including high-profile tourist attractions, outdoor excursions, sports, the arts, shopping, and dining.

Omaha's Henry Doorly Zoo has been ranked number one by *Reader's Digest* magazine. Its claims to fame include the world's largest indoor rain-forest, indoor desert, and nocturnal exhibit. It also features a drive-through zoo at its Wildlife Safari, which specializes in native environments, animals, and birds. The world-famous Girls and Boys Town, founded by Father Edward J. Flanagan in Omaha in 1917 as a home for abused and neglected boys, is a national historic landmark—and still very much in operation. The Strategic Air & Space Museum between Omaha and Lincoln displays the aircraft and history of the U.S. Air Force and Strategic Air Command. The Missouri Basin Lewis & Clark Interpretive Trail & Visitor Center in Nebraska City is the nation's only museum dedicated to the famed explorers' scientific finds. And historians, paleontologists, and regular folks are intrigued by the fossils continually unearthed at Ashfall Fossil Beds State Historical Park in northeastern Nebraska, where hundreds of prehistoric horses, camels, and rhinoceroses were fixed in time by volcanic ash some 12 million years ago.

Above: Visitors examine an SR-71 reconnaissance jet in the atrium of the Strategic Air Command Museum in Omaha. Right: Flowers are only some of the garden produce offered at the Haymarket Farmers' Market in Lincoln.

Theater and art venues abound. Besides night spots and theatrical and musical festivals, Omaha offers the ornate Orpheum Theater, the modern Holland Performing Arts Center, the Omaha Community Playhouse, the stately Joslyn Art Museum, and dozens of art galleries. Qwest Center Omaha has featured such acts as U2, Paul McCartney, and the Rolling Stones. Lincoln enjoys the Sheldon Memorial Art Gallery and Sculpture Garden, which has an expansive collection of modern art, and the Lied Center for Performing Arts. For something with a bit more of a Western feel, Ogallala's Front Street features stage shows complete with cowboys and dance-hall girls.

For outdoor adventure, it's hard to beat river rafting on the Niobrara, camping in scenic state parks and recreation areas, and biking or hiking on a myriad of trails throughout the state. There's hunting and fishing galore, amazing wildlife- and bird-watching, and, for something different, authentic western ranch experiences and covered-wagon rides.

Besides college sports of almost every variety and every competitive level throughout the state, the Omaha area features Triple A baseball team the Omaha Royals, the nationally acclaimed and followed NCAA College World Series each June, AAA hockey, arena football, and more. While golf courses pepper the whole state, *Golfweek* magazine has ranked the Sand Hills Golf Club the best modern course in the nation, and Wild Horse Golf Club near

Gothenburg in its top 25. A new course, Dismal River Club near Mullen, opened in 2006 under the design leadership of Jack Nicklaus.

Nebraska's shopping offers something for everyone. There are the famed Cabela's sportsmen's utopia in Sidney, the quaint Old Market in Omaha, and the signature Haymarket District in Lincoln. Other prairie emporiums include the homegrown St. James Marketplace, east of Wynot; Borsheims Fine Jewelry, often called the Tiffany's of the Midwest, in Omaha; and the enormous Nebraska Furniture Mart, also in Omaha.

Restaurants in the smaller towns are known for Czech, Danish, and German delicacies as well as Nebraska beef, while Omaha and Lincoln offer plenty of cosmopolitan, ethnic, and fine dining—along with, of course, big, juicy steaks.

Economic Climate

Although it has long been an agricultural and livestock leader, Nebraska balances its agrarian foundation with other industries such as transportation, insurance, and manufacturing—with food processing being the primary type of manufacturing. But its economy has now become even more diversified, with technology, health care, and tourism playing larger roles. In fact, tourism is now the third-largest revenue generator after agriculture and manufacturing. Nebraska is home to five Fortune 500 companies, including Warren Buffett's Berkshire Hathaway Corporation, all in Omaha. Many other Fortune 500 firms have major operations in the state.

Through legislated incentives, Nebraska has fostered a business climate that encourages development and start-ups. The Nebraska Advantage package, for instance, entices businesses to expand or locate in the state by offering investment and wage credits, sales tax refunds, state and

Opposite page: A corn farmer programs a computer-controlled center-pivot irrigator on the High Plains. This page, above: Eggs in Norfolk nestle in a candling tray, used to determine which eggs are fertilzed. This page, left: Nebraska eateries offer up everything from regional ethnic dishes to Omaha's famous beefsteaks.

Nebraskans enjoy a high quality of living that is propelled by such benefits as low housing costs (opposite page), excellent health care (this page, top), and top quality education (this page, bottom).

local sales tax exemptions, and tax credits for research and development, among other encouragements. In 2005, the Nebraska Legislature initiated revitalization of the rural economy by focusing on agricultural and nonagricultural entrepreneurship through tax relief and other incentives in an effort to stimulate local community development.

New residential construction and an ever-increasing number of homeowners have combined in recent years for a powerful boost to the state's economy. In Omaha, with its hefty population and business concentration, residential sales and construction are booming. The downtown area is alive with new high-rise buildings, condominiums, and entertainment facilities.

Nebraska's overall cost of living is below the national average, the median price of a home is just over $100,000, and the median rent is $540 per month. And Nebraska is the only state to have a completely public power system, which provides electricity to businesses and homes at some of the lowest rates anywhere.

Education and Health Care

Nebraska's emphasis on top quality education and health care for its citizens has paid big dividends. In 2005, Morgan Quitno ranked Nebraska as the ninth-healthiest state and the United Health Foundation ranked it 11th for overall health, noting its high rate of high school graduation and low rates of childhood poverty and uninsured people.

Morgan Quitno named Nebraska the 12th-"smartest" state in 2005, based on such criteria as student achievement and the amount of attention that teachers give their students. Nebraska's education leaders are not content with the status quo. An ongoing state initiative to improve student writing has resulted in 86 percent of Nebraska's fourth-, eighth-, and 11th-graders writing proficiently. The ACT scores of Nebraska's college-bound students have earned the state a first-place ranking among states in which 70 percent or more of students take the test.

The University of Nebraska has four campuses: Lincoln, Omaha, Kearney, and the University of Nebraska Medical Center (UNMC) in Omaha. Creighton University in Omaha is a Jesuit Catholic university with undergraduate, graduate, and professional schools and colleges, drawing students from all over the world. In the Omaha area alone, there are 15 colleges or universities, two medical schools, and four vocational/technical schools. Community colleges, satellite campuses, and video/online courses bring higher education to all parts of the state.

The two academic health centers, UNMC and Creighton University Medical Center, have associated physicians at clinics throughout the state, and research and clinical programs that earn national and international recognition. Lincoln and Omaha health care systems earn top marks in national comparisons.

Nebraska is no longer a well-kept secret. From its ancient and pioneer history, to its agricultural backbone, and into its confident future, Nebraska is on the move. But no matter where technology, economic development, and population growth may take it, Nebraska will always be centered on the land. That is the core of its diverse and big-hearted personality, the essence of its spirit.

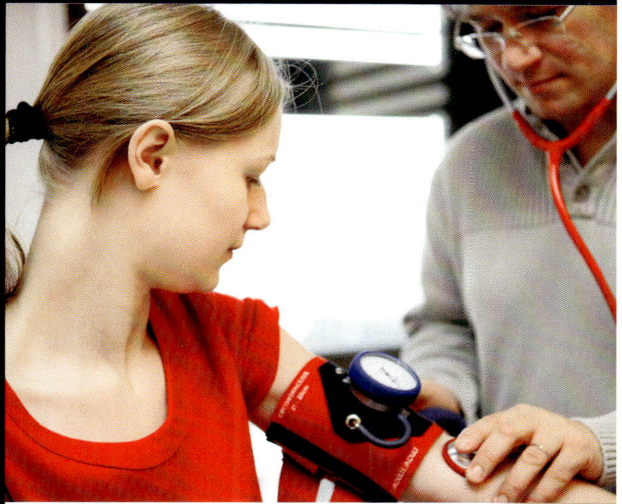

PART TWO
BLAZING NEW TRAILS: NEBRASKA BUSINESS AND INDUSTRY

BY MICHAEL GOODWIN

SOWING THE SEEDS OF GROWTH:
Agriculture

Cattle and calves (below, left) bring in better than half of Nebraska's agricultural proceeds. To feed cattle as well as people, the state grows more than 1.3 billion bushels of corn a year (opposite page), making it the nation's third-largest corn grower. Other important crops include grain sorghum (top right) and soybeans (bottom right).

There are few states in which agriculture plays as large a role in the economy as Nebraska, where cattle outnumber people four to one. Nebraska is situated on the eastern edge of what was once called the Great American Desert, which has proved to be quite the opposite—the state is at or near the top of the nation in the production of many farm commodities, and food that sprouts in Nebraska soil feeds the world. About a fifth of Nebraskans make their living in agriculture, and 93 percent of the land in Nebraska is used for farming and ranching. Nebraska's $3 billion in ranch and farm exports in 2004 generated $4.7 billion in additional economic activity when transportation, warehousing, and financing are factored in. As the industry changes, Nebraskans are responding with innovative strategies to manage natural resources, create new products, and make a career in agriculture an attractive choice for young people.

Nebraska developed into an important cattle production center in the 1870s, and its abundant supplies of water, feed grains, and pastureland have kept beef production one of the top industries in the state. There's a good reason Nebraska continues to bill itself as the Beef State: one-fifth of all steaks and hamburgers in the nation come from Nebraska, according to the Nebraska Cattlemen's Association, and more than half of Nebraska's agricultural cash receipts come from cattle or calves. Nebraska also ranks at or near the top in a number of U.S. Department of Agriculture statistical categories, from the amount of land in farms and ranches to the amount of commercial red meat produced.

This page, right: Grain silos line a rail yard in central Nebraska. Both pages: Nebraska ranks among the country's top 10 producers of pork (below) and eggs (opposite, left), and is the country's largest producer of great northern beans (opposite, right).

Other animal operations also contribute to the state's livestock strength. Nebraska is one of the top 10 pork-producing states. Hog sales generate about $800 million in sales annually and on-farm hog production alone provides the estimated equivalent of 1,700 full-time jobs. The state also ranks seventh in the nation in commercial egg production. Two-thirds of Nebraska farms have livestock or poultry operations.

While livestock accounts for a greater share of agricultural income in Nebraska, crop production is the backbone of the ag economy, serving as the primary feedstock for most animal operations as well as a major export. As it was for the homesteaders who first broke Nebraska's rich soil, corn remains the state's top crop. Nebraska farmers produce more than 1.3 billion bushels annually, ranking the state as the third-largest corn producer in the nation. About a quarter of that is fed directly to animals, while just under half is exported.

Nebraska is also a leading producer of other crops. The eastern part of Nebraska is where it raises most of its soybeans, its second most popular crop; in 2005, Nebraska ranked fifth in the country in soybean production. In other parts of the state, particularly the southeastern and south-central

The advent of groundwater irrigation, and in particular the center-pivot irrigator (right), turned the Great American Desert into the grain basket of the world. Center-pivot irrigators now dot the High Plains with their distinctive circular patterns (left).

regions, farmers grow grain sorghum, also known as milo, a hardy grain whose uses in addition to food include ethanol, feed, and packaging materials. Nebraska also produces large quantities of winter wheat and dry edible beans, especially great northern beans, which are used in soups and stews. In the Panhandle region, sugar beets are a significant cash crop and the refineries that process them are a major source of employment.

Undergirding Nebraska's agricultural success is a bounty of natural resources, particularly water. The advent of groundwater irrigation in the 1920s tapped into the state's plentiful sub-surface water supply, opening up more land to farming, increasing the land's productivity, and stabilizing grain yields by making crops less susceptible to fickle weather. About 60 percent of the Ogallala Aquifer, a natural underground reservoir that contains five times the amount of water in Lake Erie, lies beneath the state. The Nebraska Department of Agriculture estimates that if all of Nebraska's groundwater sat on the surface of the state, it would form a lake nearly 38 feet deep.

Below: Nebraska's abundance of corn makes it a natural leader in the production of ethanol, which is used as fuel in its own right or mixed with gasoline; the state is also a major producer of soybeans, which not only are nutritious but also yield a cleaner-burning, nonpetroleum diesel fuel. Right: A cropduster attacks pests in a cornfield in Saline County.

Nebraska is second in the nation in total irrigated acreage, and 43 percent of its crops are irrigated, including about 70 percent of the corn crop. A recent study estimated that irrigation had a $3.6 billion impact on Nebraska's economy in years with normal precipitation and was responsible for almost 36,000 jobs. In years of drought, the impact is even greater—45,000 jobs in 2003, for instance.

Recent drought years have heightened concerns about Nebraska's water supply for future generations. In response, the Nebraska Legislature authorized the creation of the Water Policy Task Force, which is charged with coming up with a management plan that balances the needs of surface- and groundwater users, including municipalities and wildlife areas as well as irrigators. In 2004, the Legislature passed a law that lets the state freeze new drilling permits in areas where water rights have been fully appropriated, allowing state and local officials to work together to come up with a water management plan for the area.

Nebraskans are active in diversifying the state's agricultural base with the development of new products and nontraditional commodities. A significant percentage of the state's corn crop is used in ethanol production, and researchers based at the University of Nebraska–Lincoln are studying the ethanol potential of alternative crops like switchgrass. In Blair, agribusiness giant Cargill uses

Opposite page: Rolls of hay glow in the evening light near Chadron. This page: Nebraska's once-dormant wine industry (left) has rebloomed in recent years, producing whites, reds, blushes, meads, and apple wines. Cuthills Vineyards (below) sits on 15.5 acres outside of Pierce and hosts an annual blues festival in August.

40,000 bushels of corn a day to produce a polymer that is used to make, among other things, environmentally friendly packaging. And, starting in the 1980s, the Legislature passed several bills aimed at reviving Nebraska's long-dormant wine industry. Viticulture continues to gather momentum here, with more than a dozen farm wineries producing wine from Nebraska grapes and several others planning to open in coming years. Other farmers have been experimenting with "agritourism" as an alternative income source, with hunting tours and corn mazes among the attractions.

Like other states, Nebraska is not immune to such issues as an aging population of farmers and the consolidation of its farms, but state leaders aren't letting the state's agricultural traditions go quietly. In 1999, lawmakers passed the Beginning Farmer Tax Credit Act, which gives a tax break to established farmers who rent to or partner with new farmers, helping beginners overcome the high costs of starting an operation from scratch. State leaders also went to court to try to save Initiative 300, a voter-approved ban on corporate farming, after a federal judge ruled it unconstitutional in 2005. Proponents hail the ban as one of the toughest such laws in the country.

WOODMEN

BUILDING ON A HISTORY OF STRENGTH:

Business Services

Nebraska's largest city, Omaha, is home to a thriving banking and insurance industry, as witnessed by the Woodmen and First National towers (opposite page), the iconic Mutual of Omaha building (below, left), and the commercial edifices on 15th Street (below, right) near the spot where land speculators from Council Bluffs, Iowa, took a gamble on a new territory in 1854.

Among Nebraska's many strengths is its commitment to helping businesses grow, especially industries that provide steady, well-paying jobs throughout the state. Insurance and finance; telecommunications; and engineering, architecture, and construction—these are industries Nebraska has nurtured and seen flourish. Insurance and financial institutions are especially important in Nebraska, employing more than 57,000 people between them and forming the state's sixth-largest economic sector.

Omaha's status as a regional commercial hub is enhanced by the presence of Mutual of Omaha, one of the country's largest and best-known insurers. Mutual was founded in 1909 and was the leading accident insurer in the United States by the 1950s. The Mutual of Omaha Companies' broad range of products includes life insurance and other investment products sold by its United of Omaha Life Insurance division, and health and accident policies written by its Mutual of Omaha Insurance subsidiary. Mutual reported consolidated assets of more than $18 billion in 2005. The company is also known for its conservation efforts, highlighted by the long-running *Mutual of Omaha's Wild Kingdom* television show.

Another Omaha insurer, Woodmen of the World, is one of the largest fraternal benefit societies in the United States, offering life and health coverage as well as other financial services. In 2005, the company set records for life insurance in force, investment income, and total assets. Its income for the fourth consecutive year was more than a billion dollars. Members also contributed more than 206,000 volunteer hours and $1.4 million to Hurricane Katrina relief efforts.

This page: Warren Buffett, a native Nebraskan and the second-richest man in the world, at right in glasses, applauds at the opening of the New York Stock Exchange in March 2006. Opposite page: The Nelnet logo adorns the top of the loan company's headquarters building in Lincoln.

Banking and other financial services also play a big role in Omaha. Among the largest institutions is First National Bank, a private, family-owned financial services company with 150 years of history in the area. First National Bank, which was the first bank west of the Missouri River to receive a federal charter, and which has more than 6.6 million customers nationwide and manages assets worth in excess of $17 billion, has had an impact on the Omaha skyline as well; in 2002, the First National Tower surpassed the Woodmen building as Nebraska's tallest skyscraper. Omaha is also home to TD Ameritrade, a brokerage firm that pioneered online investing. The company continues to post record earnings and win awards for top-notch customer service.

One of Nebraska's best-known companies, Berkshire Hathaway, is also headquartered in Omaha and is led by one of the world's richest men, Warren Buffet°t. While its most important operation remains property and casualty insurance, the company had 68 distinct businesses as of 2005, from Forest River, a large manufacturer of recreational vehicles, to See's Candies, a well-known producer and retailer of fine sweets. Those many businesses—as well as minority stakes in food, health products, and publishing concerns, among other interests—helped make Berkshire Hathaway the 13th-largest company in the United States, according to *Fortune* magazine's 2006 rankings.

Lincoln has also earned a reputation for companies outstanding in the financial services industries. Ameritas Life Insurance Corp., founded in 1887 as Old Line Bankers Life Insurance Company of Nebraska, was Lincoln's first local insurance company, and has since diversified into other financial products, notably dental insurance. Ameritas merged first with Acacia Life Insurance Company, and then with Union Central Life Company in January 2006 to form the UNIFI Companies, with more than 364,000 policyholders and members. UNIFI manages over $25 billion in assets and has projected annual revenues in excess of $1.6 billion. The mutual holding company is headquartered in Lincoln. Another Lincoln-based company, Nelnet, is one of the top educational lenders in the country, with more than $20 billion in assets.

In the 1980s, Omaha's location in the Central Time Zone and its proximity to Strategic Air Command (now United States Strategic Command, or USSTRATCOM) at nearby Offutt Air Force Base fueled its growth as a telemarketing center. By the mid 1990s, the telecommunications industry employed some 20,000 people in Omaha. Today, Omaha-based companies such as SITEL, an outsourcing customer-support services company with 34,000 employees worldwide, and West Corporation, which was one of the first telemarketing companies in the country and which has diversified into business services such as teleconferencing and debt collection, keep that industry humming along.

Both pages: From central boardrooms to go-anywhere high-tech start-ups, Nebraska's strong communications infrastructure is a key to unlocking business growth.

Both pages: Nebraska, and Omaha in particular, has long been a center of the global telecommunications industry, providing conferencing, debt collection, and superior voice and Internet services to North America and the world.

The bulk of telephone services in Nebraska is provided by Denver-based Qwest Communications and by ALLTEL Communications, an Arkansas company that acquired Lincoln-based Aliant Communications in 1999. A significant part of Nebraska's rural population, however, is served by small, local providers, which some experts credit with increasing the availability of broadband access in outlying areas. A survey released in 2006 indicates that 93 percent of Nebraskans have access to high-speed Internet connections via digital subscriber line (DSL), integrated services digital network (ISDN), or wireless or cable modem, and that most of the rest can access the Web via satellite. And Nebraskans are plugging in, too; a U.S. Department of Commerce study ranks Nebraska in the top half of states in terms of percentage of households connected to the Internet.

Nebraska counts on its strong communications infrastructure—as well as the presence of a skilled workforce and the availability of state funds for job training—to attract high-tech companies to the state. That combination led computer services firm Technologent to put a call center in Ainsworth, a community of 1,800 in the north-central part of the state, in 2003. As of 2005, the center had created 58 new jobs.

Nebraska architecture and engineering firms help people and companies move from the planning stages to bricks-and-mortar reality. As of 2006, there were 169 licensed engineering firms located in Nebraska and 107 architecture firms, with 22 licensed to do both engineering and architecture. Altogether, engineering, architecture, and related services in Nebraska employ more than 5,000 people and have an annual payroll of about $250 million.

Nebraska engineering firms have an earned reputation for quality, thoroughness, and creativity. Among them is HDR, headquartered in Omaha with more than 5,000 employees worldwide. In the early 1900s, HDR built its reputation designing water and sewer systems throughout the Midwest, and it helped

Below: Nebraska architecture, engineering, and construction firms are adept at custom home design and large commercial projects alike. Right: Children's Hospital of Omaha exemplifies the innovative approach to interior spaces exercised by HDR.

develop Nebraska's public power infrastructure in the 1930s. The employee-owned firm is especially adept at the design of medical facilities. *Modern Healthcare* magazine has ranked it among the top four medical design firms in the country every year since it started its rankings in 1978.

Olsson Associates, based in Lincoln, is another engineering firm that has grown steadily over time and developed a national name for itself. Since John E. Olsson launched the firm as a one-man operation in 1956, the company has expanded its services to include everything from airport design to wastewater management. Olsson Associates has offices in seven states and employs more than 500 people. The company has become a regular on *Engineering News-Record*'s list of the country's top 500 design firms, and has also been named one of the nation's best places to work by *Civil Engineering* magazine. Among its major ongoing jobs is the Antelope Valley restoration project, a long-term urban revitalization, transportation, and flood-control project in Lincoln.

Nebraska companies specializing in architecture have earned solid reputations, too. One firm whose bold designs have won it state, national, and worldwide praise is Randy Brown Architects of Omaha. Brown's innovative designs have garnered the company dozens of awards from the American Institute of Architects as well as the attention of local and national media. The firm's office was included in the *Phaidon Atlas of Contemporary World Architecture*, a 2004 book that features 1,052 buildings in 75 countries.

The construction industry in Nebraska employs more than 46,000 people and has seen substantial growth in recent years, especially in Omaha. As the urban population increases, however, declining population in outlying areas has become a concern. Some of these areas are returning to an old idea to revitalize their local economies: land give-away programs modeled on the Homestead Act of 1862. Small towns like Kenesaw and Curtis, both with populations of less than 900, have been offering free land to families who choose to move there and build a home. Communities are hoping the land grants will help people rediscover the benefits of small-town living, and Nebraskans are looking to their new homesteaders to preserve the state's rural character while moving it into a new era of prosperity.

Business Statistics

THE FOUNDATION OF FUTURE SUCCESS:

Education

Both pages: In addition to training students in the arts, the sciences, and the professions, Nebraska's public and private colleges and universities provide a base for business incubation, community leadership, and research into subjects from agriculture to virology.

Higher education in the Cornhusker State has come a long way since neighborhood cows grazed on the University of Nebraska campus in the 1880s. Nebraska now has eight state-run institutions, 16 private colleges and universities, and dozens of community college campuses and satellite locations. In addition to providing jobs for more than 26,000 people, these institutions educate Nebraska's next generation of business, industry, and community leaders.

The University of Nebraska–Lincoln (UNL), whose graduate school was the first west of the Mississippi, has long been recognized as one of the leading public research and teaching institutions of the Great Plains. The flagship of the four-campus University of Nebraska (NU) system, UNL now offers hundreds of programs to about 21,000 graduate and undergraduate students. While freshman enrollment has been down slightly in recent years, university leaders are proud to say that the overall quality of the student body is on the rise, as evidenced by the increase in average ACT scores and a high ranking in National Merit Scholars per capita. Among UNL's graduate and professional school offerings are degrees in business, law, and architecture.

As a comprehensive land-grant university, UNL blends education with outreach to touch the lives of nearly every Nebraskan. More than a dozen research centers and facilities study topics from children's social services to virology. The university's Institute of Agriculture and Natural Resources (IANR) provides formal and informal education statewide, its findings having practical applications in fields ranging from

This page, left: A volunteer discusses raptor recovery at the Nebraska Wildlife Habitat Evaluation Program. This page, right: The Technology Development Center at the UNL Technology Park offers labs and offices with the latest amenities. Opposite page: NCAA Division I-A football is only one of the amenities at the University of Nebraska–Lincoln.

drought mitigation to bioenergy. The IANR also oversees the state's 4-H program—a particular plum in that Nebraska has more 4-H members per capita than any other state. A partnership between the university's Rural Initiative and the J. D. Edwards Honors Program places interns in rural companies to encourage development through technology.

The university also has strong ties to business communities in Lincoln and elsewhere. The UNL Technology Park, a partnership with other public and private entities, allows qualifying companies access to university faculty, facilities, and other resources. On another front, the university's Bureau of Business Research performs economic modeling, forecasting, and analysis. Not to be outdone, UNL's Nebraska Center for Entrepreneurship has been recognized as one of the best and most innovative programs of its kind by the United States Association of Small Business and Entrepreneurship; hundreds of students take advantage of courses and networking opportunities through the center every year. And the university offers NU Skills, a series of online, interactive business seminars, as a convenient means of advanced training for Nebraska business people.

The NU system's other campuses have carved out solid reputations for undergraduate, graduate, and continuing education. The University of Nebraska at Omaha, one of the country's last municipal universities until it merged with the NU system in the 1960s, was a commuter college until building its first on-campus housing in the late 1990s. Now with campus housing for over 1,000 students, the school has a well-regarded undergraduate business program and has made an impact internationally with its unique Center for Afghanistan Studies, a long-standing program that assists with education and development in the Middle Eastern nation. The University of Nebraska at Kearney, which was part of the state college system until 1991, opened as a teachers college in 1905 and continues to have a strong education program, graduating 25 to 30 percent of the state's educators. The university's approximately 6,500 students can now choose from 170 undergraduate majors, 25 preprofessional programs, and 34 graduate programs. Areas of study include the university's industrial distribution program, a combination of courses in business, management, and industrial technology that is among the largest such programs in the country.

MEMORIAL·STADIUM

The Don L. Love Memorial Library stands amid its attendant gardens on the south side of campus at UNL. The Love Library, whose holdings emphasize the humanities and social sciences, is the university's main library, and is equipped with wireless network and standard Internet ports.

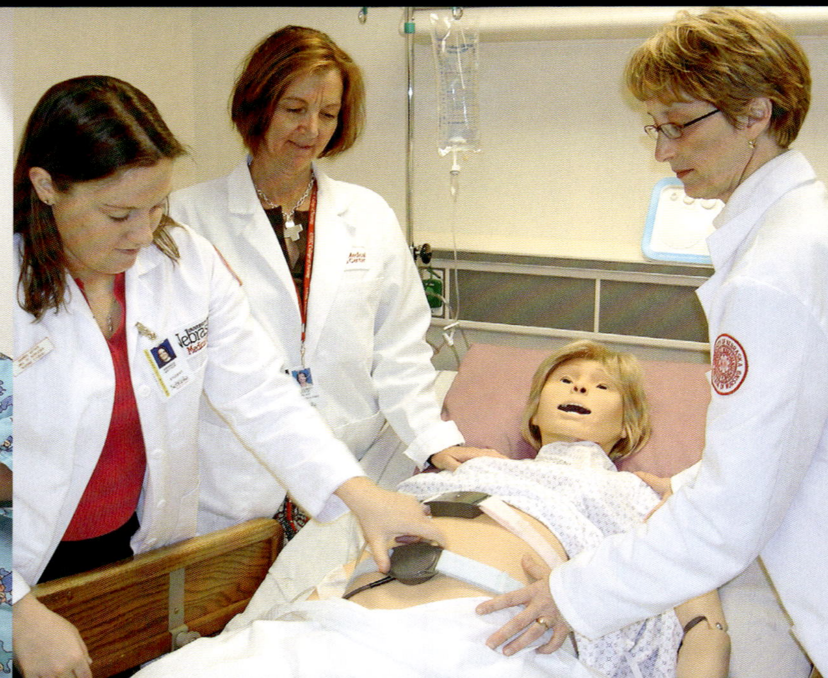

Both pages: The University of Nebraska Medical Center in Omaha features schools of medicine and nursing, and educates about half of the state's health care professionals. Its hospital merged with Clarkson Hospital in 1997, and the joint entity became known as the Nebraska Medical Center in 2003.

The University of Nebraska Medical Center (UNMC) got its start as the private Omaha Medical College in the 1880s and became part of the NU system in 1902. Officially recognized by the legislature as a separate campus in 1968, UNMC awards degrees in medicine, dentistry, pharmacy, and nursing as well as in 10 allied health professions such as medical technology and physical therapy. It graduates about half of the state's health professionals. The College of Medicine has earned national recognition for its rural health and primary care programs, and the College of Nursing offers the state's only doctoral degree in nursing. A renewed emphasis on research in the late 1990s has resulted in more than $72 million annually in external research funding to study topics from cancer treatment to bioterrorism preparedness. The NU Board of Regents recently approved plans to build a new 134,183-square-foot building to house classrooms, labs, and an events center.

The legislature chartered the state's first post-secondary institution at Peru in 1867 to train teachers, and later added campuses in Kearney, Wayne, and Chadron. Today the Peru, Wayne, and Chadron campuses make up the Nebraska State

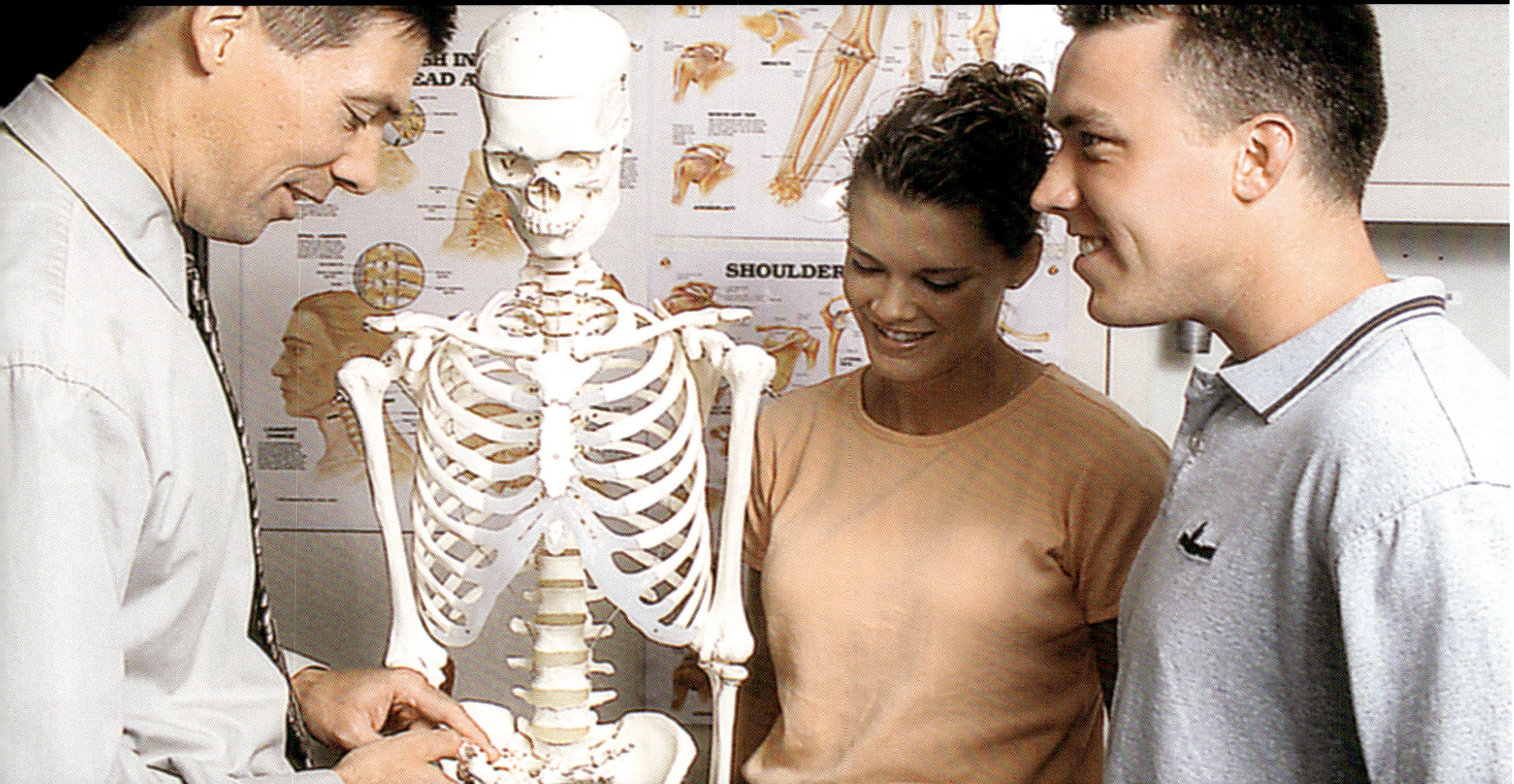
SHOULDER

Educational opportunities in the Cornhusker State range from well-regarded state and community colleges (opposite page) to private institutions like Creighton University (this page), which consistently rates among the best master's universities in the Midwest. Creighton is particularly noted for its College of Arts and Sciences.

College System. The system serves about 8,000 students and offers preprofessional programs as well as academic degrees and certificates of achievement. It also offers hundreds of online classes every year. Peru State's online master's degree program has earned national praise for its quality and affordability.

With undergraduate enrollment in Nebraska at an all-time high, several of the state's private colleges and universities have enrolled record numbers in recent years while garnering an impressive list of awards and recognitions. Nebraska Wesleyan University in Lincoln has produced more than a dozen Fulbright scholars since 1997 and a Rhodes scholar in 2005, and in recent years has attracted additional students with its graduate programs in nursing and forensic science as well as other programs designed for nontraditional students. The "teacher warranty" program at Doane College in Crete, which backs up its education graduates with continuing support in their first year of teaching, has been a model for similar programs at other colleges across the country.

Creighton University, a Jesuit institution with some 6,800 students in Omaha, has built its national reputation for excellence in the sciences. Ranked highly by *U.S. News & World Report* and the Princeton Review, Creighton boasts award-winning faculty in a variety of disciplines in addition to its science programs, which are the focus of nearly half of its students. It has the Midwest's oldest nursing school as well as Nebraska's only private law and medical schools. Creighton business and

economics professors also survey economic conditions in a region extending from Arkansas to North Dakota and publish reports used by government agencies and business professionals. In 2005, the university launched an ambitious $350 million fund-raising drive that will pay for land acquisition, upgrades for its science facilities, new residence halls, faculty endowments, and student scholarships. Creighton also has an established tradition of advanced education in pharmacology, nursing, dentistry, medicine, and other health professions. Its dentistry and pharmacy programs have also been praised for their work with low-income, uninsured, and minority patients.

With 13 major campuses and class centers in more than 300 other communities, the Nebraska Community College Association plays an important role in making higher education and job training accessible to Nebraska residents. A locally elected board governs each of the system's six regions, which have their own customized workforce-training programs with classes available both on- and off-site for everything from soldering to Spanish.

Trauma
ED
Access

AT THE HEART OF A HEALTHY ECONOMY:
Health Care and Biosciences

Both pages: From teaching hospitals to centers of innovative surgical techniques, Nebraska's health care institutions promote public wellness, create jobs, and train the physicians of the future.

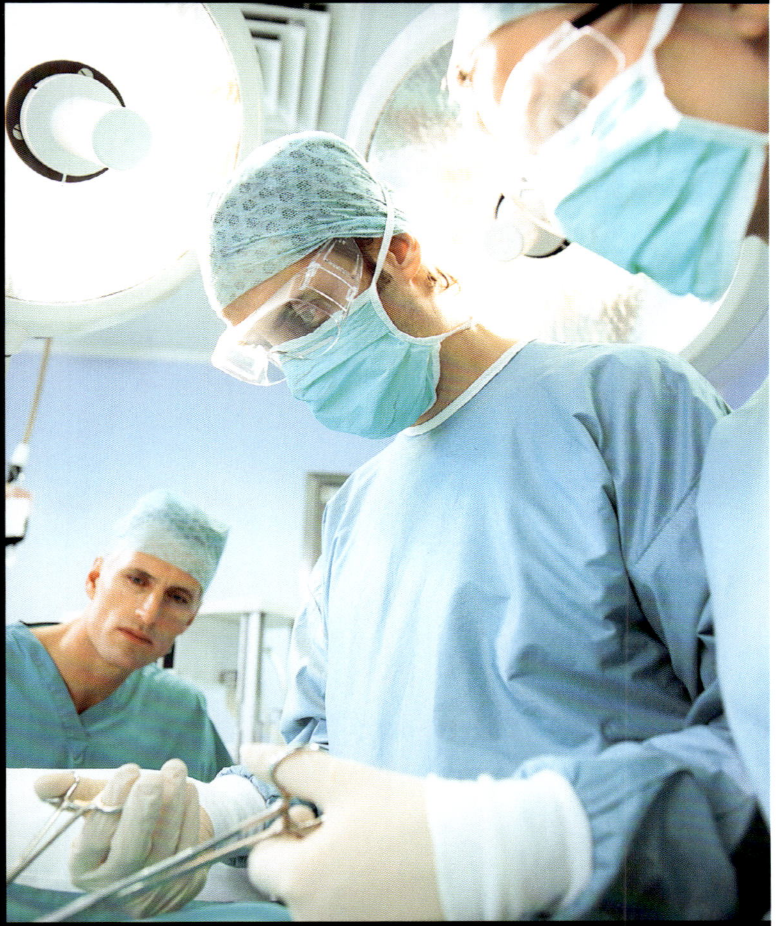

A robust health care sector is important not just for overall public wellness but also for the many high-paying jobs the industry creates. According to federal statistics, health care employs almost 13 percent of Nebraska's workforce, and prospects for growth are good as the state's population grows and ages.

Omaha is a health care and medical research hub not only for Nebraska but the nation as well. The city has two medical schools as well as numerous hospitals with solid reputations for quality patient care. Among the top is the not-for-profit Nebraska Medical Center (NMC), a 689-bed teaching hospital formed in 1997 when Nebraska's first hospital, Clarkson Hospital, merged its hospital and clinical operations with the University of Nebraska Medical Center (UNMC). Known for excellent all-around medical care as well as innovative cancer treatment and organ and bone marrow transplantation, the hospital in 2005 was awarded the coveted J. D. Power and Associates Distinguished Hospital award. The award, which is based on the quality of patients' experiences, is given to only 20 percent of hospitals in the country. Important cooperative ventures between UNMC and NMC include the Lied Transplant Center, which has transplant clinics and labs as well as on-campus lodging so that family members of organ recipients from Nebraska and beyond can be trained as partners in caregiving.

The highly regarded medical center at Creighton University in Omaha has research teams focused on bioterrorism, cancer biology, inflammatory diseases, hereditary cancer, hearing loss, and osteoporosis. The Creighton Cancer Center performs research and clinical care for breast cancer and skin cancer. Doctors at the center have also helped develop a better way to treat peritoneal carcinomatosis, a form of cancer that spreads tumors over the surfaces and linings of the abdominal cavity and its organs.

In addition to employing thousands of people at their hospitals and medical schools, Nebraska health care facilities generate job growth through their research divisions. UNMC researchers, who nearly tripled their external research funding between 1996 and 2005, estimate that every million dollars of research funding translates into roughly 34 new jobs for the state, both inside and outside of the institution.

Creighton recently completed a $56 million upgrade to its laboratories, which are used by students, faculty, and health care professionals, and the Boys Town National Research Hospital in downtown Omaha has one of the largest research facilities in the world devoted to childhood hearing loss and other communication disorders.

Complementing hospital research are independent research companies like Streck, Inc., which develops and sells hematology controls and other lab products. The company has earned dozens of patents in more than three

Medical research in Nebraska spans the realms of oncology, osteoporosis, and burn treatment at the state's medical schools (opposite, left); pediatric hearing loss, as at Boys Town National Research Hospital (opposite, right); and commercial applications discovered at labs both public and private (below).

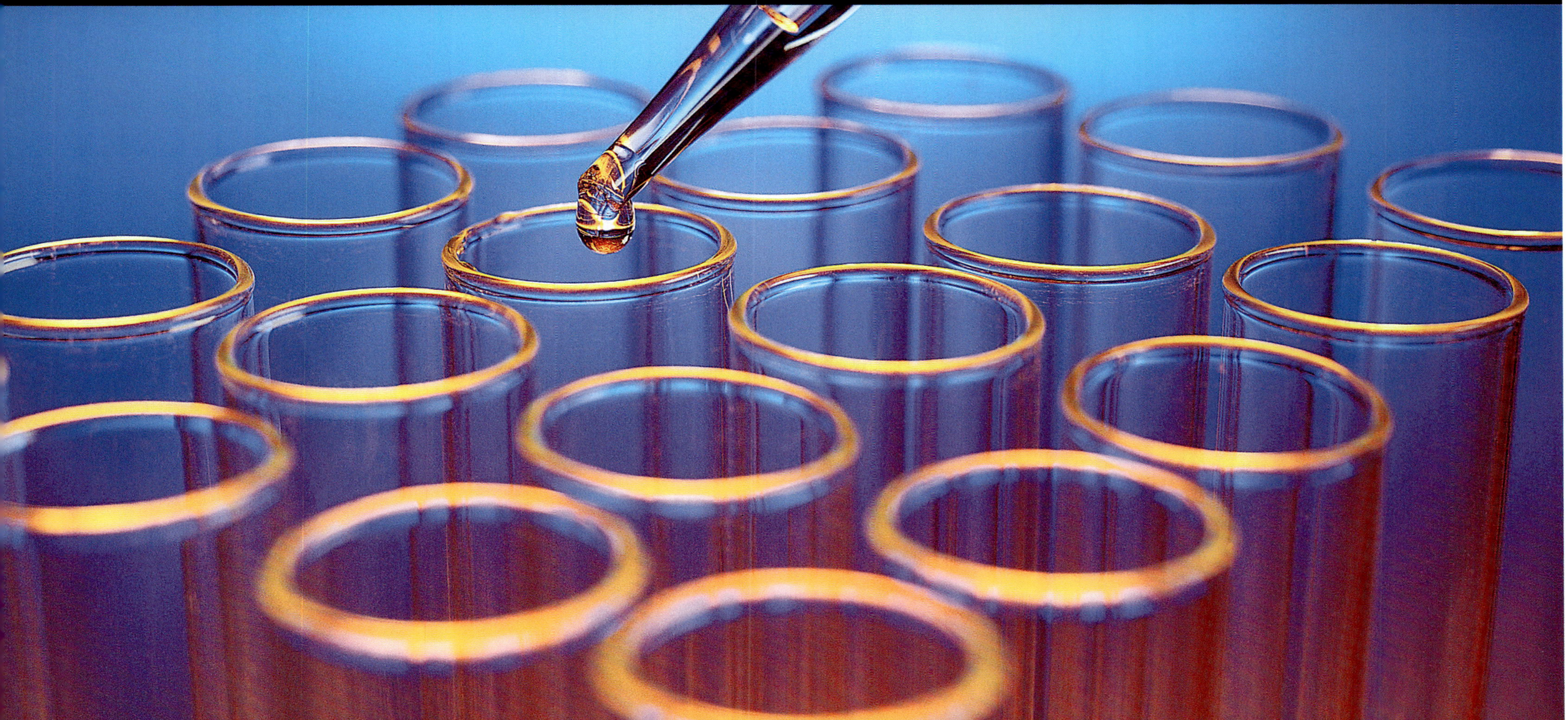

The University of Nebraska Medical Center and the Nebraska Medical Center campus in Omaha, from the Durham Outpatient Center (at center) to the Lied Transplant Center (at far right), is an important hub of clinical excellence as well as far-reaching research into the nature of neurodegenerative diseases such as multiple sclerosis and Alzheimer's disease.

UNIVERSITY HOUSE
OUTPATIENT SURGERY

Lakeside

Opposite page: Lakeside Hospital at Lakeside HealthPark in west Omaha is Alegent Health's most recent addition. This page: The imaging facilities at Lakeside, such as this magnetic resonance imager (MRI), increase diagnostic speed and accuracy while minimizing patient discomfort.

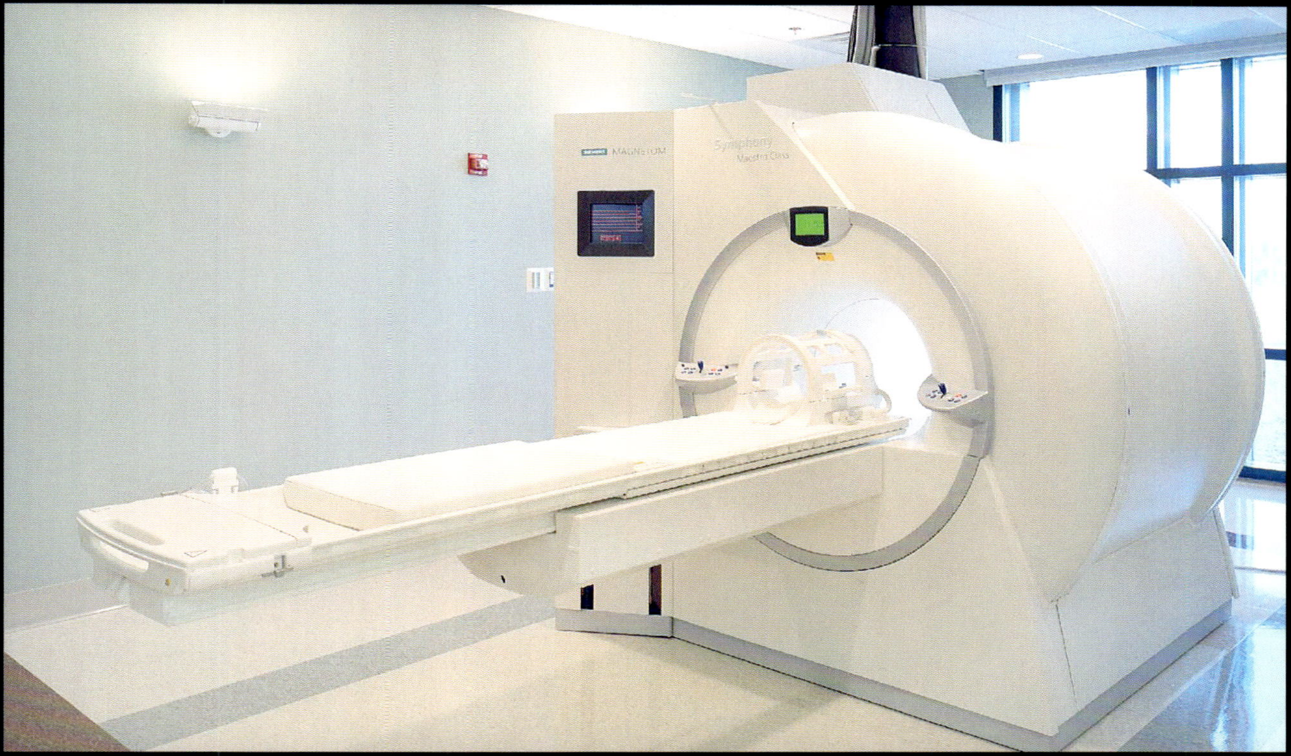

decades in business, and currently has a 65 percent share of the world market in hematology controls.

The union between Catholic Health Initiatives and Immanuel Health Systems created Alegent Health, a regional health care network with nine hospitals and more than 1,200 physicians. The network's nine acute care hospitals have earned a host of awards, especially for bone and joint replacement. Alegent Health was also named in *Modern Healthcare* magazine's list of the top 100 integrated health care systems for six of the seven years between 1998 and 2004. A 2003 survey named the system's hospitals as among the best places to work in Omaha. The newest Alegent facility, Lakeside Hospital, is already expanding; the hospital added a fourth floor in 2005, less than a year after it opened.

Lincoln's hospitals have enviable reputations and a list of awards to prove it. Bryan Memorial Hospital and Lincoln General Hospital merged in 1997 to create BryanLGH Health System, which includes two full-service campuses and the BryanLGH College of Health Sciences. Together the two campuses have beds for about 600. The college offers degrees in nursing, sonography, and cardiovascular technology. In 2001, the system embarked on the largest private hospital expansion in Lincoln's history. The six-year, $183 million expansion project will include a new emergency trauma center, conference center, and patient room enhancements.

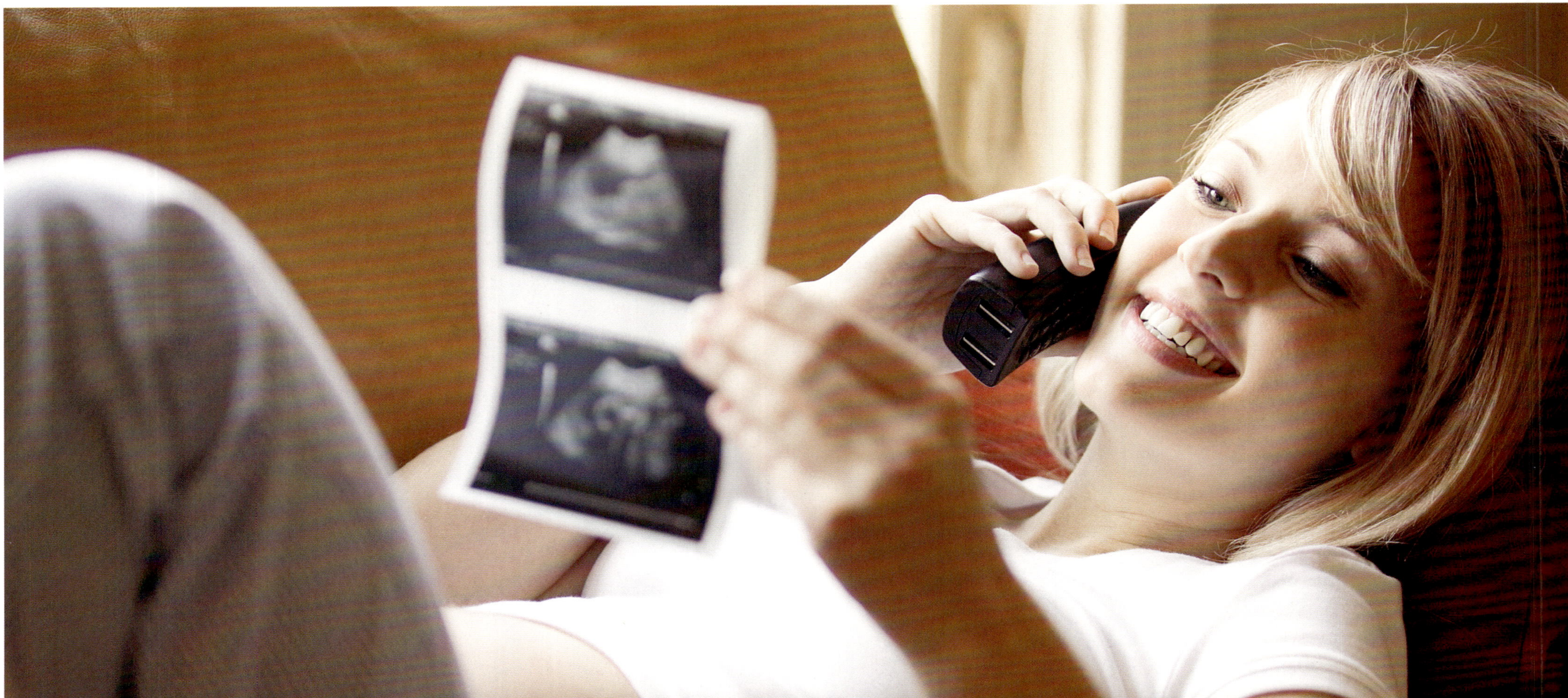

The 242-bed Saint Elizabeth Regional Medical Center is also in the midst of expansion, with a new patient tower, medical office building, and parking garage going up on its east Lincoln campus. The hospital, which was Lincoln's first, is today a corporate partner with Catholic Health Initiatives, the second-largest Catholic health care system in the country. The Saint Elizabeth Regional Burn and Wound Care Center, the only burn center in the region when it opened in 1973, is one of two in Nebraska to be accredited by the American Burn Association. (The other is at the Nebraska Medical Center.) The expertise of the burn center staff has been requested at disaster scenes all over the country, including the World Trade Center after the attacks of September 11, 2001.

Nebraska hospitals, medical centers, and research facilities are noted for their excellence. Saint Elizabeth has made the prestigious Solucient 100 Top Hospitals list three times in recent years. Also appearing on the list are Creighton University Medical Center and Alegent Health Bergan Mercy

Both pages: Whether in obstetrics, geriatrics, or pediatrics, Nebraskans are in good hands at every stage of their lives.

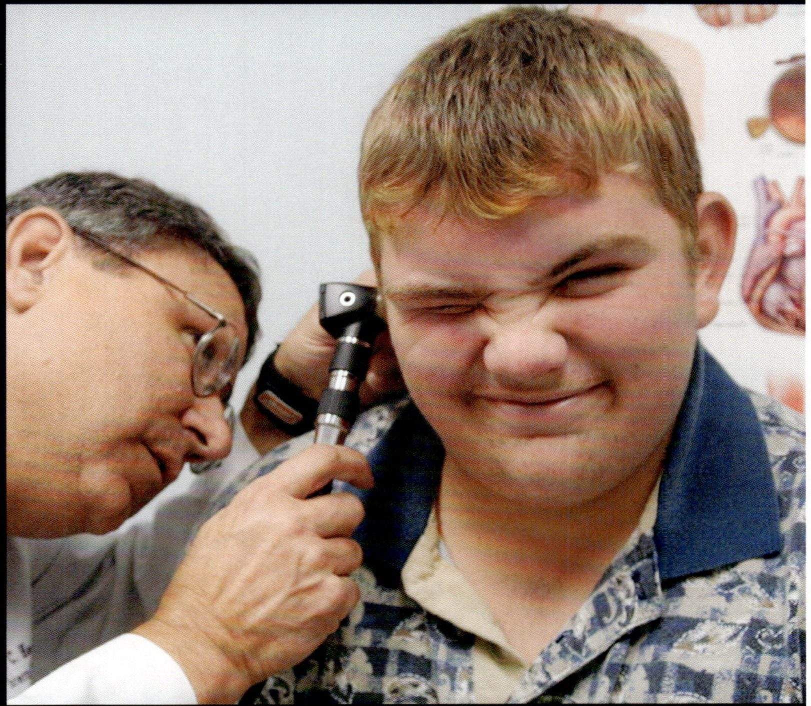

Medical Center in Omaha, Niobrara Valley Hospital in Lynch, and BryanLGH Medical Center in Lincoln. BryanLGH's clinical programs have been consistently ranked in the top 10 percent in the nation for cardiac and orthopedic services by Health Grades, a national health care quality company that has also given top marks to Regional West Medical Center in Scottsbluff and Methodist Hospital in Omaha. Methodist Hospital and Saint Elizabeth have earned magnet status from the American Nurses Credentialing Center, a designation that recognizes excellence in nursing care and job satisfaction.

Even as medical services in urban areas grew in scope and availability, finding enough health care professionals to serve Nebraska's rural population was problematic. To address the issue, UNMC launched its Rural Health Education Network in the early 1990s with the goal of encouraging its graduates to settle in outlying areas by providing part of their clinical education there. The program's mission later expanded to encourage high school students in rural areas to consider careers in health care. The initiative also led to the Rural Health Opportunities Program (RHOP), which allows students at Wayne State College and Chadron State College to obtain early admission into a number of UNMC programs. More than 70 percent of RHOP graduates go on to provide health care services in rural areas.

MADE IN NEBRASKA:

Manufacturing and Food Production

Opposite page: Production in Nebraska ranges from mountains of grain to the silos necessary for storing it. This page: Meatpacker Tyson Foods maintains a sizeable presence in Nebraska, along with Cargill, Farmland Foods, Archer Daniels Midland, and the culinary giant of Omaha, ConAgra Foods.

The manufacturing industry in Nebraska has always had strong ties to agriculture and has become one of the state's largest employers, with more than 103,000 workers. Some companies started in places like Grand Island and Deshler and grew into global leaders while remaining anchors of their local economies. The Omaha metro area, however, continues to be the state's manufacturing center.

Food processing dominates the Nebraska manufacturing scene, especially animal slaughter and processing, which employs 73 percent of the state's 37,000 food-manufacturing workers. Omaha's proximity to both corn and cattle country, not to mention its railroad access, encouraged the growth of its stockyards in the 1880s, and the city has been an important meatpacking center ever since. As of the 2002 economic census, the city had almost three dozen animal slaughtering and processing facilities that employed some 7,000 workers.

One meat processor with a considerable Nebraska presence is Arkansas-based Tyson Foods, a Fortune 500 company with about 9,000 employees in Nebraska. The company, one of the world's largest processors of meat products, expanded the beef facility at its Dakota City plant in March 2006, a move expected

Both pages: Nebraska is a noted food processor, from its famous beef, such as these juicy T-bones (below) from Omaha Steaks, Inc., to such pantry mainstays as Chef Boyardee canned pasta (opposite) by ConAgra.

to increase its beef production by 6 percent. It also maintains plants in Lexington, Madison, Omaha, and York.

Food industry giants such as Cargill, Farmland Foods, and Archer Daniels Midland have a large presence in the state, but small, locally owned companies have carved out niches in the competitive food industry. MBA Poultry, for example, was the first American company to use purified cold air instead of water immersion to chill its birds, a process designed to preserve the meat's natural flavors and reduce the risk of bacterial contamination. MBA's signature product, sold under the name Smart Chicken, is available in 39 states. MBA announced plans in 2005 to build a new packaging and distribution plant and corporate office facility in Waverly while keeping its initial processing operation in Tecumseh, where the company was founded in 1998.

Other Nebraska companies are leaders in processed foods, notably Omaha-based ConAgra Foods. ConAgra—a Fortune 500 company—and its subsidiaries make several of the world's most recognizable consumer brands as well as products for the food service industry. Known as Nebraska Consolidated Mills until 1971, the company reported net sales of more than $14.5 billion for the 2005 fiscal year. In recent years, ConAgra has focused on branded prepackaged foods, which now account for about 85 percent of sales. An estimated 96 percent of American homes have ConAgra products in them, and many of the company's brands, including Chef Boyardee canned pasta, Wesson cooking oils, and Hunt's tomato products, are among the nation's best sellers. ConAgra continues to explore new areas of food service; in 2005, the company introduced a line of products designed to look and taste like they are made with refined flour while having the nutritional value of whole grains.

The Nebraska agriculture industry can attribute much of its success to center-pivot irrigation, a concept developed within the state's borders. In essence a self-propelled water pipe that rotates around a fixed point, a center-pivot irrigator conserves water, saves labor, and allows fields of uneven topography to be irrigated, opening up more land to cultivation and mitigating the effects of drought. Nebraska has more center-pivot users than any other state, and several homegrown companies have capitalized on the success of the center pivot to build worldwide clienteles.

Valmont Industries is the largest of those companies. It started out making farm elevators and other farm equipment in 1946 near the small town of Valley, and licensed the patent for the first center pivot in 1954. By the 1970s, it was a player on the international scene, selling agricultural equipment on every continent except Antarctica. Today, the Omaha-based company has 43 operations in

EASY OPEN TOP
Chef
BOYARDEE
BEEF
Ravioli
In Tomato & Meat Sauce
Nutrition Facts

Both photos: A fortuitous confluence of corn, cattle, and the transcontinental railroad, which linked the coasts via its eastern terminus in Omaha, made Nebraska an important meatpacking center in the 19th century. The state remains such today, with its steaks and chops appearing in supermarkets and boutique groceries around the world.

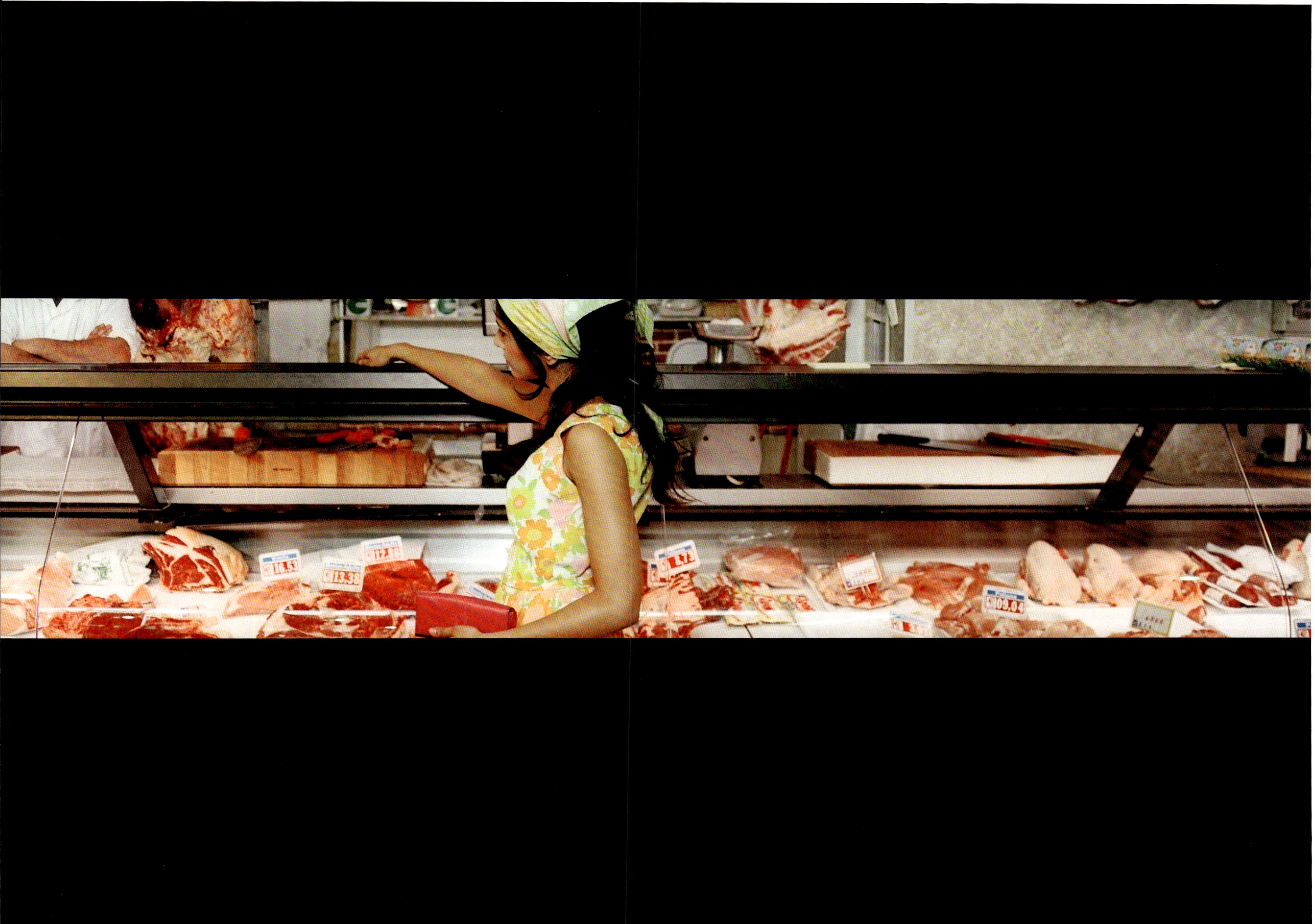

Metal fabrication (opposite page) plays a vital role in Nebraska industry, finding applications particularly in agriculture, such as steel storage sheds and silos (this page, left) to irrigation equipment (this page, right).

14 countries and employs more than 5,600 people, including about 1,500 in Nebraska. Other important irrigation manufacturers based in Nebraska are Lindsay Manufacturing in Lindsay, T-L Irrigation in Hastings, and Reinke Manufacturing in Deshler.

Even Nebraska's pharmaceuticals industry spends a good deal of its energy on agricultural concerns. More than half of the state's pharmaceutical manufacturers make products for animals, and these companies are a mix of large, international operations such as Pfizer and Schering-Plough and smaller firms such as Pharma Chemie in Syracuse. Pharma Chemie makes products sold under some of the pharmaceutical world's best-known names, including Bayer and Eli Lilly.

Not all manufacturing in Nebraska relates to agriculture. However, true to the state's midwestern character, its workforce aims for quality and thoroughness in whatever it does. Firms making items as diverse as metal buildings and electrical components have found Nebraska an ideal location.

This page: A Chief Industries bucket elevator, built by the company's Agri/Industrial division in Kearney, lifts grain at a farmers cooperative in southwest Nebraska. Opposite page: Attention to detail makes Molex's Lincoln plant a globally competitive maker of electrical connectors for Ford, Sony, IBM, and other customers.

Metal fabrication is an important part of Nebraska's economic landscape, occupying about 9 percent of the manufacturing workforce. About 300 metal fabrication firms in Nebraska make everything from tools to buildings. Grand Island's Chief Buildings leads the metal-buildings field. Chief's buildings have a number of applications and are distributed through a network of 300 builders across the United States. The parent company, Chief Industries, started as a construction firm in 1954 but has since diversified into factory-built homes, transportation equipment, and ethanol production, among other areas. It also makes King of the Road recreational vehicles. The company has distribution and manufacturing facilities in Nebraska and six other states as well as in England and France.

The high-tech business of electrical equipment and components is also a big part of the Nebraska industrial economy, with about 4,000 employees at 29 firms in 2002. One such company, Molex, added about 100 jobs to its Lincoln plant in 2005 to bring its number of employees there to 800. The company is the world's second-largest maker of electronic and fiber-optic connections used in products from cars to refrigerators to wireless phones. Although the Lincoln plant is just one of 115 Molex facilities across the world, company officials cite its integrated operations and its employee work ethic as making it globally competitive.

In 2005, Nebraska lawmakers renewed their commitment to keep the state's economy strong with an updated business incentive package that includes a sales tax exemption for manufacturing equipment. The legislative package, dubbed the Nebraska Advantage, includes $15 million for job training assistance as well as tax credits for companies that create specified numbers of jobs and invest in research and development. The new laws are expected to help others discover what many companies and consumers have known for decades: Nebraska-made products are among the best in the world.

UNION PACIFIC
9553

CHARGING AHEAD:

Transportation and Energy

Opposite page: A Union Pacific freight train balls the jack through Sheldon. This page: A bronze statue in Marysville commemorates the short-lived but legendary Pony Express.

Even before the transcontinental railroad laid its tracks across Nebraska's vast expanse, the area had a history as a major transportation corridor. Thousands of travelers on the Oregon Trail, Mormon Trail, and the Pony Express route passed through what would later become Nebraska. Today, Nebraska's central geographic location, combined with its historically low utility rates, puts the state's trade and transportation sectors in an advantageous position.

Good highways are particularly important in a large state like Nebraska. The state was the first to finish its portion of the interstate highway system, embedding a ceremonial brass link six miles west of Sidney in 1974 to signify the completion of Interstate 80. Stretching from New Jersey to San Francisco, I-80 connects Nebraska from one end to the other and is one of the two busiest east-west routes in the country. Travelers on I-80 spend the bulk of the tourism dollars spent in Nebraska; and much of the state's 8 percent population growth between 1990 and 2000 occurred in counties along the highway's 455-mile stretch, a pattern that is expected to continue. A 10-year project to widen the interstate to six lanes between Lincoln and Omaha is scheduled to be completed in 2012.

This page, left: A summer thunderstorm passes over Highway 2 in the Sand Hills. This page, right: A construction crew installs a guardrail at the junction of I-80 and I-76, just north of the Colorado state line near Big Springs. Opposite page: Omaha's Werner Enterprises, with some 9,000 tractors and nearly 25,000 trailers, is one of the largest trucking firms in the country.

While the interstate carries 21 percent of vehicle traffic in Nebraska, its rural highways are an important part of the transportation infrastructure as well. The Nebraska Department of Roads allocates roughly half of its state and federal construction dollars to state highways, with the other half divided evenly between the interstate and four-lane expressway system. In 1988, the state set a goal of connecting its mid-size cities with 600 miles of four-lane expressway. Through the 2006 fiscal year, that expressway system was 68 percent complete. Nebraska has made major improvements in the quality of its road system; in 1994, 54 percent of state roads were rated "good" or "very good." By 2003, that percentage had improved to 84 percent.

Nebraska's low population density makes for uncongested roadways, which is good for the state's trucking industry. Trucks carry about three-quarters of inbound manufactured freight in Nebraska, and the trucking industry employs about 7 percent of the workforce. About 85 percent of the U.S. population is within a two-day drive, based on truckers' current hours-of-service laws. Nebraska is served by about 8,000 licensed motor carriers, ranging from large, publicly traded corporations to small, single-truck operations. Major firms include Werner Enterprises, an Omaha-based Fortune 1,000 company with terminals throughout the country, and Crete Carrier Corporation of Lincoln, one of the largest privately held carrier groups in the United States. Both companies are listed among *Inbound Logistics* magazine's top 100 motor carriers.

Gavin's Point Dam, which impounds Lewis & Clark Lake on the Missouri River in northeastern Nebraska, provides hydroelectric power, a reliable water supply, and recreational boating and fishing. The stretch below the dam is one of the last wild sections of the Missouri.

Like other western territories, Nebraska depended on the railroad for development, and train tracks remain an important conduit for freight, particularly agricultural commodities. The state ranked third in farm products transported by rail in 2004, carrying just over 10 percent of the nation's total. The railroad industry is also a significant part of the state's economy; more than 12,000 Nebraskans make their living working for the railroad, putting the state behind only Texas and Illinois in terms of railroad employment. On average, these employees earn yearly wages of $67,700. Nebraska is also served by Amtrak's *California Zephyr* trains, which make five stops per day in each direction on their way between the San Francisco Bay area and Chicago.

The development of the railroad industry has played a significant role in the history of Omaha, the headquarters for the Union Pacific Corporation. The company helped complete the first transcontinental railroad in 1869. Today, Union Pacific Corporation is a Fortune 500 company, and its chief subsidiary, Union Pacific Railroad, is the largest railroad in North America, serving 23 states and connecting the major ports of the Pacific and Gulf coasts. Added together, Union Pacific and Burlington Northern Santa Fe control 2,726 miles of tracks, about three-fourths of the total miles of

Opposite page, above: Amtrak's *California Zephyr* moves through Nebraska twice daily. Opposite page, below: A United Express CRJ-200 taxis down runway 32 at Lincoln Airport. This page, left and center: Union Pacific operates both a railroad museum and the world's largest classification yard in North Platte. This page, below: A tug works a pair of barges along the Missouri River.

tracks in the state. North Platte is home to Union Pacific's Bailey Yard, which is about the size of 2,800 football fields and is the world's largest railroad classification yard. An estimated 135 trains pass through the yard every day, carrying coal, food, chemicals, and other goods to points all over the continent.

Other modes of transport play a smaller, though still important, role in Nebraska's transportation infrastructure. The Missouri River, which runs along the state's eastern border, is the only route for waterborne commerce in the state, providing a way to get exports like sand, gravel, and farm products to ports on the Gulf Coast quickly and cheaply. While the bulk of commercial airline activity is in Lincoln and Omaha, regional airports offer nonstop service to Denver, Chicago, Minneapolis, and other large cities, and dozens of local airstrips dot the landscape for private plane use.

The setting sun silhouettes power lines in Sherman County (opposite page). Nebraska Public Power District provides power at rates significantly lower than the national average. The district's generating facilities range from natural gas–fired plants like the one at Beatrice (this page, top) to wind farms (this page, bottom).

As a major producer of agricultural commodities, Nebraska has the potential to become what one official called "the Saudi Arabia of biorenewables," especially with federal mandates aimed at doubling the nation's biofuel production by 2012. About a third of the state's corn crop goes into ethanol annually, and with each plant's dependence on local grain for raw material, farmers often see a rise in income when an ethanol plant is built nearby. At more than a billion gallons a year, Nebraska already has the nation's second-highest ethanol production capacity.

Nebraska has the most extensive public power system in the nation, with almost 100 percent of residential and commercial users getting their power from a publicly owned utility. This means that the state's residents traditionally enjoy rates significantly lower than the national average. More than 150 different utilities provide electricity, with many locally or regionally operated systems purchasing power from the Nebraska Public Power District (NPPD), a subdivision of the state government that covers all but two of the state's 93 counties. NPPD's generating facilities include nuclear, hydroelectric, and wind facilities in addition to several diesel and steam plants. Natural gas, which about 70 percent of Nebraskans use for heat, is supplied by a mix of public utilities and private companies at prices that are among the lowest in the country.

PART THREE
PORTRAITS OF SUCCESS: PROFILES OF CORPORATIONS AND ORGANIZATIONS

WOODMEN

PROFILES OF COMPANIES AND ORGANIZATIONS

Nebraska Cities

Enduring vision, high standards, and a long-standing partnership between public and private leaders have established Omaha as a city of the present and future, with great opportunities for economic success and an overall excellent quality of life.

Above left: Standing tall in the middle of Omaha's beautiful downtown skyline is the First National Bank Tower. Above right: Qwest Center Omaha, a state-of-the-art convention center and arena, offers a 194,000-square-foot exhibition hall and a 17,000-seat arena.

By consciously planning for growth, fostering competitive economic development, and providing residents with effective and efficient city services, Omaha distinguishes itself as one of the country's best places in which to live, work, and play.

Omaha, Nebraska, because of its vision and teamwork, has become the envy of cities nationwide. This modern metropolitan area boasts an economic climate in which any business or citizen can succeed—just ask any of the four Fortune 500 companies that call Omaha home. And the city's unique public-private partnerships ensure that Omaha continues its march to an even brighter future.

With a current metropolitan population of 800,000, Omaha is a AAA-bonded economic leader in telecommunications, health services, transportation, and defense. Most recently, Omaha rebuilt its downtown and Missouri Riverfront with a $2 billion reinvestment. Omahans and visitors alike enjoy the transformation that now includes the First National Bank Tower, the Qwest Center Omaha Convention Center and Arena, the Lewis & Clark Landing, the Holland Performing Arts Center, Gallup University, ConAgra Foods, and the Carl T. Curtis National Park Service Midwest Regional Headquarters.

Innovative urban design continues to set Omaha apart. As one of the largest initiatives of its kind ever undertaken by a city in the United States, "Omaha By Design" is a comprehensive urban development program that ensures the city is built to higher standards, which include the promotion of streetscapes, neighborhood preservation, pedestrian-friendly connectors, and overall design guidelines.

Additionally, City of Omaha leaders have worked closely with neighborhood and business leaders to craft individual economic development plans for the revitalization of Omaha's smaller business districts. To ensure that the community as a whole runs smoothly and efficiently, city government also supports scores of municipal services; a dozen different departments, including public works, parks, tourism, police, and fire; and half a dozen city-related agencies such as the Douglas Omaha Technology Commission and the Keep Omaha Beautiful, Inc. organization.

In little more than 150 years, Omaha has grown from a small ferry stop on the banks of the Missouri River into one of the most prosperous cities in America. Its success combines many factors, not the least of which is a long history of progressive public and private sector leaders who have embraced the promise of the city's present and future.

OMAHA'S
ROSENBLATT STADIUM

PROFILES OF COMPANIES AND ORGANIZATIONS

Agriculture and Food Production/Processing

ConAgra Foods, Inc.

With a history in Nebraska that goes back to 1867, ConAgra Foods, Inc. is as committed as ever to producing the foods that consumers love and maintaining the expertise that customers value, while remaining a company that cares for the land and its communities.

Above: Located at 10th and Farnam streets in downtown Omaha, the ConAgra Foods, Inc. campus is home to the company's corporate headquarters, research and development center, and Consumer Foods and Commercial Products business units.

ConAgra Foods, Inc. (NYSE: CAG) is one of North America's largest packaged food companies, with a strong presence in consumer grocery, as well as in restaurants and food service establishments. As a leader in multiple segments of the food business, ConAgra Foods understands what consumers want: familiar brands, favorite foods, and innovative products that make meals and snacks great-tasting, convenient, and affordable.

Since its first bag of flour was sold in 1867, ConAgra Foods has grown from a small Nebraska company into one of America's largest food companies. ConAgra Foods is headquartered in Omaha, with administrative centers in Minneapolis, Chicago, Boise, and Toronto, and manufacturing plants across the United States.

More than 95 percent of refrigerators, freezers, or pantries in the homes of American families contain a ConAgra Foods product, from Hunt's® tomatoes and Chef Boyardee® pasta to Orville Redenbacher's® Gourmet® Microwave Popping Corn, Hebrew National® hot dogs, Healthy Choice® frozen meals, and Reddi-wip® topping. Even most of America's top restaurant chains use ConAgra Foods products.

However, ConAgra Foods does not measure success based on the kind of food it makes. Instead, the company concentrates on meeting the varied tastes and nutritional needs of every type of consumer, at every stage of life. When it comes to food trends, ConAgra Foods doesn't follow them, but anticipates them, therefore emerging as a leader in shaping what America eats.

ConAgra Foods operates two business segments: Consumer Foods and Commercial Products. Each segment provides strength to the other.

ConAgra Foods Consumer Foods provides the brands people know and love that are sold through grocery, convenience, and club stores. ConAgra Foods Commercial Products offers innovative solutions to the restaurant and food service industries. Combining insights in consumer behavior and tastes with an insider's knowledge of its customers' businesses means that ConAgra Foods is more than just a vendor; it is an invaluable partner that provides its customers with the edge needed to succeed in today's competitive food industry.

Whether counting calories, grams of fat, or carbohydrates, consumers across

the country rely on ConAgra Foods to provide a variety of nutritious and tasty foods—everything from Healthy Choice frozen meals and PAM® cooking sprays to the recently introduced organic products from Hunt's and Orville Redenbacher's. The company even produces a line of meatless, soy-based vegetarian products under the Lightlife® label.

ConAgra Foods also brings the same level of dedication and innovation to improving the communities in which its employees live and work. Within the company's own operations, thousands of ConAgra Foods employees work to promote environmental stewardship and profitable growth through the company's Sustainable Development program. The program's goal is to improve production processes by introducing new technologies that reduce waste and conserve energy and water. As a result of various sustainable development efforts, the company has cut operating costs and has reduced its consumption of natural resources.

The company's charitable division, the ConAgra Foods Foundation, assists dozens of projects around the country, from disaster relief to flood safety education. One of its signature programs, Feeding Children Better, specifically targets childhood hunger in the United States through a partnership with America's Second Harvest. Currently, Feeding Children Better is the nation's largest corporate initiative dedicated to eliminating childhood hunger.

The ConAgra Foods Foundation funds cultural, environmental, and educational projects throughout Nebraska and the United States. Through its support of the Iain Nicolson Audubon Center at Rowe Sanctuary in Nebraska's Platte River Valley, the foundation is helping restore and conserve a vital habitat for sandhill cranes and other wildlife along the Platte River, as well as educating children and adults about the importance of this vital ecosystem. Additionally, the foundation's funding of the Nature Conservancy has proved vital to conservation efforts along the Platte, helping establish farming practices that keep the land in production with minimal impact on the river's health.

ConAgra Foods also serves as the presenting sponsor of some of Omaha's best-known events, including the Holiday Lights Festival and New Year's Eve fireworks celebration held on the ConAgra Foods campus, the holiday ice sculpture display, and the Race for the Kids one-mile run/walk,which promotes physical fitness for children.

Whether providing the foods that help keep consumers happy and healthy or the energy and funds that sustain local land and communities, ConAgra Foods embodies the philosophy of "doing well by doing good"—the only way the company believes in doing business.

Above left: ConAgra Foods products are found in virtually every aisle at grocery stores and are appropriate for any meal or occasion. Above right: ConAgra Foods serves as the presenting sponsor for some of Omaha's most popular events, such as the Holiday Lights Festival and the New Year's Eve fireworks celebration, which lights the sky over Heartland of America Park.

Greater Omaha Packing Co., Inc.

Uncompromising in food quality and safety since 1920, this family-owned beef processing company in the heart of America's cattle country ships its products around the world, sustaining Nebraska's reputation for premium beef.

Above: From its 300,000-square-foot, state-of-the-art plant in South Omaha, Greater Omaha Packing Co., Inc. provides some of the highest quality beef in the world.

Herman Cohen founded Greater Omaha Packing Co., Inc. in 1920. This family-owned beef processor operation was located at the center of what was then the world's largest livestock market. Throughout the years and technological changes, the company has continued to play an integral role in making Omaha and Nebraska famous for quality beef.

Premier International Supplier

Today, Greater Omaha Packing not only is one of the largest privately owned beef processing companies in the United States, it is internationally recognized as a premier supplier of beef worldwide. In fact, the company's products are shipped throughout Japan, Korea, Indonesia, China, South America, Mexico, Canada, Russia, and Egypt. Greater Omaha Packing is also one of the few U.S. plants that is allowed to export beef into restrictive European Union markets, which is a definite symbol of quality in this industry.

Headquartered in a 300,000-square-foot, state-of-the-art plant near the historic livestock exchange building in South Omaha, Greater Omaha Packing also has a distribution center in Denver, Colorado, and it runs an export operation in San Bruno, California. Altogether, it employs 800 people and achieves almost one billion dollars in annual sales.

Known for Uncompromising Quality and Safety Standards

Greater Omaha Packing's success results from its commitment to quality, food safety, and customer service. The company offers consistently premium products, thanks to its long-term relationships with quality cattle producers and its "single-plant production" system. Limiting production to one plant, where all the employees follow uniform guidelines and safety measures, ensures constant, high quality standards.

To give customers the most consistently tender and flavorful products, the company became a licensed processor of both Certified Hereford and Certified Angus Beef. Hereford and Angus cattle are prized for their superior quality and taste. Today, Greater Omaha Packing processes almost 100,000 Herefords and 500,000 Angus per year.

Since health-conscious consumers demand leaner cuts of beef, Greater Omaha Packing's expert butchers closely trim products per each customer's exact specifications. To ensure food safety, the company uses 12 steps to eliminate pathogens and other contaminants. These steps include using controlled atmosphere, steam vacuums, hot water pasteurization, and acid rinse cabinets.

Committed to Exceptional, Reliable Service

At the heart of Greater Omaha Packing's service is its ability to chill and deliver product to its customers. A 60,000-square-foot refrigerated warehouse, part of the South Omaha site, efficiently chills products and readies them for delivery. Forklift-mounted computer terminals are operated by each forklift operator to log products in and out, ensuring precise inventory control. This and the company's central location enable next-day shipping anywhere in the Midwest and second-day shipping to the West and East coasts.

Greater Omaha Packing is indeed the strength behind Omaha's reputation for the highest quality, finest beef in the world.

PROFILES OF COMPANIES AND ORGANIZATIONS

Education

Creighton University

This world-class Jesuit, Catholic university in the heart of Omaha provides a values-based education with an array of undergraduate, graduate, and professional studies, and includes a noted medical school and extensive research endeavors, such as advanced cancer research.

Above left: Creighton University is located on a 130-acre campus in Omaha, Nebraska. Above right: Creighton has a graduation rate of 69 percent, placing it among the top 4 percent of colleges and universities nationwide.

Creighton University is a leading Jesuit university rooted in the Catholic tradition and is known for its welcoming Midwestern atmosphere and academic excellence. It is set in thriving Omaha, which has a healthy economy and a population of 800,000. Creighton is consistently ranked at or near the top in *U.S.News & World Report*'s "America's Best Colleges" edition among Midwestern master's universities. The magazine also lists Creighton as a Best Value, where students receive the best return on their tuition investment. The school's 6,800 students come from every state and more than 40 countries. It has an intimate, small-class environment with a 12-to-one student-faculty ratio. Creighton is distinct among Catholic universities, continually receiving national recognition for mentoring undergraduate research that leads to scholarly papers presented on campus and at national conventions.

Creighton offers more than 50 undergraduate majors in arts and sciences, business administration, and nursing, as well as 30 graduate and professional programs in law, medicine, dentistry, pharmacy, physical therapy, and occupational therapy. The university's graduation rate is 69 percent, which places it among the top 4 percent of colleges and universities in the nation. Of the degrees awarded, many are for graduate or professional degrees in 48 disciplines.

The university is also home to one of the area's leading academic medical centers, where excellent patient care, teaching, and research are the focus. Creighton University Medical Center is the site of the Creighton Cancer Center and the Hereditary Cancer Center, believed to be the nation's only cancer registry that tracks all forms of hereditary cancer. Building on research that began at the university during the 1950s, the Osteoporosis Research Center is world-renowned for its study of bone health and osteoporosis prevention, diagnosis, and treatment.

Since 1892, Creighton physicians and researchers have been significant contributors to national health care and educational advancements. Creighton scientists are dedicated to developing new therapies that improve the health and well-being of patients. By following the Jesuit, Catholic tradition of caring for the whole person—mind, body, and spirit—the university has established itself as a respected source of health care and education in Omaha and throughout the Midwest.

Dedicated to the Total Student

The university is committed to excellence in its nine undergraduate, graduate,

and professional schools and colleges. In Creighton's mission statement, members of its community are challenged to reflect on transcendent values, including their relationship with God, in an atmosphere of freedom, with core values of service, family, individual worth, and an appreciation of diversity.

The Creighton education is focused on the development of the total person, with dedication to the intellectual, social, spiritual, physical, and recreational aspects of students' lives and to the promotion of justice. It educates men and women to be leaders in their professions and to be of service to society. Annually, Creighton students, faculty, staff, and alumni provide 58,000 hours of community service locally, nationally, and abroad.

Creighton University was founded in 1878, when the Creighton College of Arts and Sciences, the school's oldest and largest division, was established. The university is named for Omaha pioneer Edward Creighton, the person largely responsible for laying telegraph lines to the West Coast and the ultimate establishment of telegraphic communication across the nation. When his wife, Mary Lucretia Wareham Creighton, inherited his fortune, she willed $100,000 to establish a school in her husband's memory.

Edward's younger brother John established the John A. Creighton Medical College in 1892, including the 200-bed Creighton Memorial St. Joseph Hospital (the forerunner to today's Creighton University Medical Center), which continues to be the main source of clinical instruction for the medical school. Between 1904 and 1928, the university's Schools of Law, Dentistry, Pharmacy, Nursing, and Graduate Studies and the College of Business Administration were established.

An Integrated Vision

Today, Creighton is a national leader in preparing students for responsible leadership, professional distinction, and committed citizenship. Its NCAA Division I athletic program includes a variety of successful varsity sports for men and women. With a 95 percent graduation rate for student athletes, Creighton is tied for 15th among all NCAA Division I schools.

The university's well-landscaped, 130-acre campus includes several facilities added since 2003, including the Hixson-Lied Science Building which increased research capacity by one-third and provides the high-tech equipment and modern laboratories necessary for science education today; Davis Square and Opus Hall junior and senior townhomes; and the 5,000-seat Morrison Stadium, home to Creighton's highly acclaimed men's and women's soccer programs.

In 2005, the university launched its most ambitious private fund-raising program to date, "Willing to Lead: The Campaign for Creighton University." This $350 million campaign is designed to provide the private support needed to fulfill the university's aspirations. The campaign is an opportunity to demonstrate that Creighton is prepared to believe, innovate, grow, excel, serve, dream, and boldly lead the way— to maintain its place among the finest Jesuit, Catholic universities in the nation and ensure its future vitality.

Left: Ngwarsungu Chiwengo, Ph.D., a native of the Congo, teaches African and world literature at Creighton University. Top left: Chemistry professor Bruce Mattson, Ph.D., works with students Sehr Haroon (left) and Jenny Gross. Creighton is a national leader in science education and research. Top center: Fans cheer on the Creighton Bluejays at one of the finest soccer facilities in the nation—Morrison Stadium. Top right: On Creighton's award-winning, refurbished campus mall is Creighton president the Reverend John P. Schlegel, SJ, with university students.

The Nebraska Community College Association (NCCA)

Created to advance Nebraska's community colleges and promote the welfare of their areas, this nonprofit corporation provides coordination services among the college districts and between the college system and other state agencies, including planning, budgeting, assessing program needs, and more.

Above: The Nebraska Community College Association coordinates and represents the state's community colleges, including Western Nebraska Community College (left) and Southeast Community College (right).

The Nebraska Community College Association (NCCA) has been representing the governing boards of Nebraska's six community college areas since 1975. The NCCA works to ensure that each individual college district remains locally governed and to maintain a funding partnership between the state, the local communities, and the students.

The Nebraska community colleges encompass 13 campuses, several centers, and more than 270 sites across the state and serve over 152,000 people.

The colleges are public, two-year, postsecondary institutions that are student-centered, have open access, and are affordable. There are three top priorities to guide them in their mission:

- Priority One: The community colleges are dedicated to providing top quality technology and occupations education. The colleges will continually grow and become more diverse while maintaining the highest quality programs in occupational education.
- Priority Two: The community colleges will offer transfer education and will work to ensure that credits are transferable to four-year educational institutions. In some of the more sparsely populated areas of Nebraska, these colleges offer the best local opportunities for postsecondary education.
- Priority Three: The community colleges will serve their districts, providing many opportunities for adult learners to obtain or enhance job skills with custom-tailored training programs. The colleges will aid in economic development activities all across Nebraska through partnerships with numerous local businesses and industries.

The NCCA and Nebraska's community colleges are proud of the reputation the colleges have established as being among the fastest growing and most responsive public postsecondary educational institutions in the state. They will continue to expand their role in economic development activities and to be prepared for any other responsibilities their local communities might present to them.

Metropolitan Community College

With six locations in eastern Nebraska, this comprehensive public community college, which opened in 1974, lets students choose from more than 100 quality programs of study, both occupational and academic, that enable them to graduate with the confidence and skills they need to compete in the modern job market.

Nebraska's largest community college and third-largest postsecondary school, Metropolitan Community College (MCC) offers more than 100 programs of study in 30 departments, including industrial and construction technologies, business, culinary arts, electronics, social sciences, and visual arts. The Higher Learning Commission (HLC) of the North Central Association of Colleges and Schools has "enthusiastically and unanimously" accredited MCC.

More than 26,000 credit students and nearly 20,000 noncredit students attend the college. Funded by taxes, MCC serves four neighboring counties in eastern Nebraska: Dodge, Douglas, Sarpy, and Washington. Its six locations—three campuses in Omaha, including the Fort Omaha campus (built on a 19th-century army outpost), the South Omaha campus, and the Elkhorn Valley campus; and three educational centers, including the Offutt Air Force Base Center in Bellevue, the Fremont Center in Fremont, and the Sarpy Center in La Vista—offer affordable courses in which students are groomed to be competitive in their careers.

MCC encompasses the resources of a large urban school combined with the warmth of a small-town college. During one-year or two-year programs, students learn by doing; MCC has the facilities that students need for hands-on education in endeavors from automotive trades to gastronomy to nursing and many other career fields.

MCC's Fort Omaha campus has 82,000 square feet of modern classrooms and laboratories spread throughout 73 acres and 32 buildings that retain the original fort's frontier architecture. The South Omaha campus, the most populous MCC location, has a 58,000-square-foot Industrial Training Center (ITC) where faculty members conduct occupational training and workshops. The Elkhorn Valley campus is steadily growing in enrollment as the Omaha area continues to expand westward. A single building set on 51 acres, the Elkhorn Valley campus offers all of the advantages of its counterparts—modern classrooms, labs, art studios, student services, and more. The college provides state-of-the-art computer labs and three libraries.

The MCC faculty believes in the integrity of each student and guarantees everyone the opportunity to master a chosen field. At the Career Network Centers, students can locate jobs, make career choices, and polish their résumés, cover letters, and interview skills. MCC's Cooperative Education Program offers internships and practicum programs, letting students apply their learning at local businesses to help them later enter the workforce with confidence.

Every year MCC educates a potential workforce that can compete globally. Even so, many MCC graduates choose to stay in Nebraska, helping to create long-term economic growth for the state.

Founded in 1974 by an act of the Nebraska legislature, MCC remains locally governed, and college leadership can add or modify programs as demand dictates. This flexibility means more choice, value, and quality for students.

Above: One of Metropolitan Community College's six locations, the 73-acre Fort Omaha campus offers modern classrooms, computer laboratories, library, art studios, student services, and more.

College of Saint Mary

Established in Nebraska in 1923, this esteemed private Catholic college offers students the unique opportunity to learn and grow in an all-women environment, to develop their potential through excellent academics, and to realize their strengths in real-world experiences.

Above left: The College of Saint Mary (CSM) offers an excellent higher education for women, who graduate to pursue excellence in their chosen professions, from the arts to the sciences. Above center: CSM's wealth of offerings includes professors who bring the best of themselves to the classroom. Above right: To facilitate the education of all women, CSM offers residence halls for single mothers, who shine as role models for their children.

The College of Saint Mary (CSM) is a Catholic college dedicated to the education of women in an environment that calls forth potential and fosters leadership. CSM's distinctive programs and offerings include an elementary education major with hands-on teaching exposure in the sophomore year; a Distinguished Scholars program for juniors and seniors that provides real-life research opportunities with faculty members; one of the area's most high-tech learning environments for nursing and occupational therapy students; a separate residence hall for single mothers and their children; and an innovative master of science program in nursing that is designed to help solve the allied health faculty shortage in Nebraska and throughout the country.

Offering Academic and Experiential Excellence

In classrooms at CSM's main campus in Omaha and at its satellite campus in Lincoln, students learn in a technologically rich and spiritually nourishing atmosphere. CSM augments its quality undergraduate and graduate programs with studies in music, theater, and art; team participation in competitive intercollegiate sports; leadership studies and experiences; and a myriad of community service activities. Beyond the classroom, Omaha's five locally based Fortune 500 companies and other organizations provide real-world learning through a host of CSM-affiliated internships and job opportunities.

Since the college's founding by the Sisters of Mercy in 1923, CSM's well-rounded education has produced intelligent, questioning women who achieve success in their careers and aspirations. Like its alumnae, CSM is always reaching for new goals—milestones that will enhance its mission of inspiring women to be valuable, productive leaders in the world.

"The College of Saint Mary is poised for phenomenal growth," states Dr. Maryanne Stevens, RSM, president of the college. "Our graduate programs in high-need areas for Nebraska will open new opportunities for students and provide committed, skilled professionals for our communities."

Additional information is available on the College of Saint Mary's Web site at www.csm.edu.

3
3
6
5
4
4
kWh

PROFILES OF COMPANIES AND ORGANIZATIONS

Energy

Working in partnership with the state's rural public power districts, cooperatives, and municipalities, Nebraska Public Power District helps to provide an estimated one million Nebraskans with electric power and energy-related services.

Above: Nebraska Public Power District (NPPD) works around the clock to provide the low-cost, reliable energy that its customers deserve and have come to expect. Part of this commitment means making investments in the utility's infrastructure to ensure that customers' needs are met for the long term.

Few services touch consumers' lives like electricity. As the state's largest electric-generating utility, Nebraska Public Power District (NPPD) understands how the service it provides impacts the quality of life of its customers. The utility was founded on the premise that all people—particularly those in rural parts of the country—should have access to the same electric services as those in more urban areas.

This belief is evident in Nebraska, the only state in the nation with electric service provided entirely by public power utilities. Governed by boards elected by the people they serve, public power serves Nebraskans well. Revenues generated above the utility's normal operating expenses are reinvested into its system or returned to customers in the form of lower rates. As a result, customers in the state benefit from paying electricity rates today that are more than 20 percent below the national average.

Headquartered in Columbus, Nebraska, and operating in a vast chartered service territory including all or parts of 91 of Nebraska's 93 counties, NPPD relies on the teamwork of its 2,100 employees located across the state to meet customer needs and expectations. One way this is accomplished is by maintaining a clear focus on the district's key mission to safely generate and deliver low-cost reliable energy and provide outstanding customer service.

This mission gives NPPD colleagues the daily direction they need to do their jobs effectively and cost-efficiently, while providing a framework for how the utility operates for the future. It advocates the need for being proactive while seeking long-term solutions that ensure customers are heard and receive what they deserve—the safe delivery of an essential commodity at rates that are fair, reasonable, and nondiscriminatory. Because the district is a political subdivision of the state of Nebraska, meeting this objective is not simply a goal—it is a requirement.

Successful completion of the district's mission begins by setting and reviewing annual strategic business strategies and adhering to a solid energy supply plan. For NPPD, this plan includes relying on a diverse mix of generating facilities to provide a stable and consistent supply of electricity to its customers.

NPPD strengthened its power reliability with the addition of two new generation resources in 2005. Beatrice Power Station, a 250-megawatt natural gas facility that went online in January 2005, was built to meet future load growth in NPPD's service area, add diversity to the district's energy fuel mix, and serve as a hedge against unexpected interruption of generation at one of NPPD's other plants. It was the first power plant built by NPPD since 1982.

The district expanded its renewable energy portfolio in October 2005, when it began commercial operation of a 60-megawatt wind energy facility (the state's largest), located near Ainsworth in north-central Nebraska. The addition of these two facilities brings NPPD's total available generation capacity to more than 3,100 megawatts.

NPPD's largest generating facility is Gerald Gentleman Station, a coal-fired facility in western Nebraska, which consistently ranks as one of the lowest-cost coal-fired generating plants in the country. The district also relies on generation from a second coal plant, Sheldon Station, as well as a nuclear facility, Cooper Nuclear Station, located in southeast Nebraska. Other resources include a 119-megawatt natural gas–fired plant, nine hydro facilities, nine diesel plants, and three peaking units. NPPD also purchases hydropower from the Western Area Power

Administration, which is operated by the federal government.

As another reliability measure, NPPD is connected to other regional utilities as a member of the Mid-Continent Area Power Pool. More than 5,000 miles of transmission lines make up NPPD's electrical grid system, which delivers power to about one million Nebraskans.

Besides competitive electric rates, local control, and reliable service, NPPD also supports local and state economic development efforts to bring jobs and growth to communities. NPPD's strategic plan includes a commitment to help build the economy of Nebraska. One of the plan's objectives is to protect and promote the proven benefits of being an all-public-power state through NPPD operations, economic development activities, and community and governmental relations.

NPPD's Economic Development Team works with leaders in communities and rural areas to ensure they are the best informed, best organized, and best prepared in their economic development efforts. This is done by helping existing businesses expand and assisting new businesses with site-location decisions.

NPPD's nationally recognized economic development Web site (sites.nppd.com) provides easy access to site-location data. NPPD has developed a statewide community profile system known as Nebraska Economic Development Information, or NEDI Online. This tool provides instantaneous access to economic and demographic information about Nebraska communities. NPPD also maintains databases of available industrial sites and buildings, helps communities create Web sites for economic development purposes, and develops promotional materials on their behalf.

Another way NPPD assists with economic development activities is by participating in local, regional, and state economic development councils and related agencies, actively providing community partners with technical and volunteer assistance.

NPPD's primary economic development targets include the food processing, plastics, and ethanol industries; distribution and warehousing facilities; and the information services industry. NPPD's economic development team also supports existing businesses and industries in its service area and encourages companies to expand their Nebraska operations.

Recognizing ethanol's potential to revitalize Nebraska's rural areas, NPPD introduced a new service in 2005 to help producers lower their energy costs. NPPD's Energy Center Services program focuses on the systems that provide steam for fuel-grade ethanol plants that use coal as their energy supply. This program also supports the district's vision of enhancing the quality of life for Nebraskans through NPPD's people and its public power assets.

NPPD serves the total wholesale power requirements of 52 municipalities and 24 public power districts and cooperatives. In addition to community commitment, NPPD routinely meets with its wholesale and retail customers to discuss rates and other issues of importance. NPPD's retail customers have the convenience of service provided 24 hours a day, seven days a week. At least 15 other utilities also benefit from the district's after-hours call-answering and/or dispatching service.

As Nebraskans serving Nebraskans, NPPD's involvement goes beyond building the economy. The district works to enhance the quality of life in the communities it serves by providing additional services such as energy education with schools and consumer groups, participating in civic groups, taking leadership roles in community organizations, and serving as firefighters and emergency medical technicians.

In the years to come, Nebraska Public Power District will be relentless in its pursuit of excellence while finding opportunities to work in harmony with others with similar interests. Remaining steadfast to its roots as a public power utility, the district will remain true to its corporate slogan to be "Always there when you need us."

Above left: Growing Nebraska's rural communities is important to the state's livelihood and is enhanced through support and attraction of one of the fastest growing industry segments—ethanol production, as at this ethanol plant near Central City. Above right: Recognizing that reliance upon any one fuel source is risky, NPPD invests in a diverse fuel mix of hydro, coal, natural gas, wind, and nuclear power. The addition of new facilities like this 60-megawatt wind farm near Ainsworth, Nebraska, enhances NPPD's system stability while expanding its renewable energy portfolio.

As one of the largest publicly owned electric utilities in the United States, this company meets the growing energy demands of southeast Nebraska with a combination of old-fashioned hard work, state-of-the-art forecasting tools, and insight based on close customer relationships.

Above: Omaha Public Power District (OPPD) is a publicly owned, business-managed electric utility that serves more customers per year than any other electric utility in Nebraska.

Business and residential customers alike tend to take electricity for granted. Their first and foremost concern is simple: "Will the light go on when I flip the switch?"

Omaha Public Power District (OPPD), which serves more customers than any other utility in Nebraska, takes the responsibility of power service, along with its reputation for dependability and value, very seriously. It regularly polls its residential customers, analyzes the results, and continually seeks new methods to increase customer satisfaction.

Clearly, OPPD is doing something right. Between 2000 and 2005, OPPD averaged 99.98 percent reliability—one of the highest results in the industry, according to the Average Service Availability Index. In 2006, for the sixth consecutive year, J. D. Power and Associates ranked OPPD first in residential customer satisfaction for midsized utilities. Perhaps further powering its high customer satisfaction standing, OPPD's rates are more than 20 percent below the national average.

W. Gary Gates, OPPD president and chief executive officer, states, "Today, while other energy costs are rising, customers expect more from their energy provider. OPPD has maintained rates that are well below the national average, and we remain committed to maintaining that cost advantage for our customers."

Initial Spark

OPPD is a publicly owned, business-managed electric utility. A self-supporting subdivision of state government, it is managed by a publicly elected board of directors that establishes policies and rates based on a business approach of not just meeting, but exceeding customer expectations.

This utility traces its origins back to 1917, when the Nebraska Power Company was incorporated and acquired the Omaha Electric Light and Power Company. By 1946, Nebraska Power Company had grown to serve more than 83,507 customers and had a generating capability of 119,000 kilowatts. That same year, the Nebraska Legislature created the Omaha Public Power District, which then acquired the properties operated by the Nebraska Power Company. Then, in 1965, OPPD merged with the Eastern Nebraska Public Power District, doubling its service area to its current size.

Power for Today and Tomorrow

Today OPPD serves 725,000 people in a 5,000-square-mile territory that includes 53 communities and surrounding rural areas in 13 southeast Nebraska counties. In addition to its headquarters in Omaha, OPPD

has three base-load power plants that provide the majority of the power: North Omaha and Nebraska City Stations, which are both coal-fired, and Fort Calhoun Nuclear Station. These plants are augmented by three peaking plants and two renewable-energy facilities, a landfill gas–fueled plant, and a wind-turbine unit.

Since energy is such a critical component of everyone's lives, OPPD is continually challenged to meet the growing energy demands of its flourishing service territory. In 2005 it began upgrading and replacing systems in its nuclear plant, Fort Calhoun Station. These upgrades have prepared the facility to produce emission-free power through 2033.

OPPD also began construction of a second coal-fired plant in Nebraska City. This new 663-megawatt facility, which will be located next to the existing 646-megawatt coal-fired plant, will use state-of-the-art multipollution controls. With completion targeted for 2009, OPPD plans to use half of the energy for its own customers and share the remaining power with seven other public power entities.

Fueled by Core Values

OPPD's success is founded on its core values: accountability, excellence, commitment to its communities, teamwork, family orientation, and safety. The first three of these values are evidenced in the utility's reliability and high level of customer satisfaction. OPPD continually demonstrates its commitment to its customers and communities through a variety of activities. Whether having employees help build a Habitat for Humanity home or acting as a leader in recycling, OPPD is dedicated to the people and towns it serves. Its Power Drive program is a statewide, nationally recognized program through which high school students design and construct safe, energy-efficient electric vehicles. OPPD's tree program provides education on the proper selection and placement of trees for beautification and conservation. Additionally, OPPD works with schools, rural communities, and businesses to educate them and help them implement more energy-efficient applications.

Safety remains a consistent and important priority to OPPD. As of August 2006, the more than 300 employees who run and maintain OPPD fossil-fuel power plants and peaking units surpassed 1.2 million hours without a lost-time injury.

Gates concludes, "At OPPD, we are committed to helping our customers succeed by providing affordable and reliable power and professional energy services. We understand our role in ensuring that Omaha and southeast Nebraska have the power to grow and thrive."

Above left: Omaha Public Power District (OPPD), supports the energy needs of southeast Nebraskans every day. Replacements and upgrades to OPPD's Fort Calhoun Station, shown here, have prepared this facility to produce emission-free power through 2033. Above right: One Nebraska family in Omaha is realizing the American dream in their own home, thanks to Habitat for Humanity and OPPD employees.

True to its motto—'Providing Energy for Better Living'—this leading natural gas company has contributed greatly to the economic development of the state of Nebraska and to the quality of life within the state's communities for more than seven decades.

Above: Natural gas is delivered safely and reliably to more than 100 communities in the eastern third of Nebraska. As new subdivisions are created, Aquila employees install new natural gas lines to serve the needs of the residents.

Aquila

Providing Energy For Better Living.℠

Aquila, Inc. has delivered safe, reliable, and competitively priced natural gas along with related products and services to Nebraska homes and businesses for more than 75 years. In addition to providing many years of natural gas utility service to Nebraska communities, Aquila has also supported the state's economic development and its community activities.

Aquila began serving Nebraska communities in 1930 as Peoples Natural Gas, the retail division of Northern Natural Gas. In 1985 UtiliCorp United acquired Peoples Natural Gas. Then in 1992 UtiliCorp United purchased Minnegasco's Nebraska natural gas utility operations. In 2002 UtiliCorp United changed its name to Aquila.

Safe, Reliable Service

Today Aquila serves more than 196,000 customers in 110 eastern Nebraska communities. Aquila's state headquarters is located in Lincoln, which is also home to one of the company's two call and dispatch centers. Several departments that support Aquila's five-state operations—in Nebraska as well as Colorado, Iowa, Kansas, and Missouri—are located in Omaha, including the company's Gas Supply Services, Gas Engineering, and Regulatory Affairs departments.

Aquila has piloted programs in Nebraska such as its Energy Options program, under which Aquila offers commercial and industrial customers the opportunity to purchase natural gas from a third-party provider. Aquila also offers an Annual Price Option program (formerly known as Fixed Price Option in Lincoln) that allows Nebraska residential customers to have a more predictable monthly natural gas bill.

Supporting Its Communities

In addition to its decades-long service as a natural gas provider, Aquila also has a tradition of strong community involvement in the areas of youth development, education, literacy, human services, economic development, and the environment. As one example of Aquila's community commitment, the Aquila Cares program matches customer donations to provide energy assistance through the Salvation Army HeatShare program. The company's employees also are active in community organizations, donating their time and talents to help make their communities better places in which to live.

Aquila, Inc. is proud to partner with Nebraskans and to earn their trust 24 hours a day, seven days a week.

VALID
THRU

PROFILES OF COMPANIES AND ORGANIZATIONS

Financial and Insurance Services

This insurance and financial services company serves customers throughout the United States and Canada, helping people manage the risks of everyday life, recover from the unexpected, and realize their dreams—one customer at a time.

Above left: George J. Mecherle founded State Farm® Insurance Companies in 1922. Above right and inset: State Farm's Lincoln Operations Center, located at 84th and O streets in Lincoln, Nebraska, processes work for the company's six-state Heartland Zone, serving Nebraska, Iowa, Minnesota, North Dakota, South Dakota, and Wisconsin.

State Farm® Insurance Companies provides insurance and financial services to more than 27 million households and small businesses in the United States and Canada. Approximately 69,000 employees, along with nearly 17,000 agents and their 60,000 staff members, share State Farm's vision to be the customer's first and best choice.

The State Farm Story

At age 22, George J. Mecherle started farming his own land near Bloomington, Illinois. In 1901 he married Edith Mae Perry, who joined him on his farm. Within a few years, he was one of the leading farmers in the area.

After the couple had farmed for 20 years, Edith Mecherle's health began to fail, and she and George decided to move to Bloomington. Unable to sit still, George Mecherle accepted a job selling insurance for a small company. He was successful as a salesman, but he didn't feel the rates or the business practices of the company suited the needs of farmers.

When he suggested a better way to sell insurance, his employer laughed and said, "If you think you have such a good idea, why don't you start your own company?" So he did. Mecherle believed that farmers should pay less for insurance because they drove less and had fewer losses than folks living in cities. Using this idea, he started State Farm in 1922 as a mutual automobile insurance company owned by its policyholders.

By 1928, the decision was made to decentralize, and the company began opening branch offices throughout the country in order to bring service closer to the customer. The Lincoln, Nebraska, office was opened in 1947 on the corner of 10th and O streets, staffed by 100 employees who transferred from company headquarters in Bloomington to Lincoln and by 100 local residents.

Today, State Farm's Lincoln Operations Center, located at the corner of 84th and O streets, serves as headquarters for State Farm's six-state Heartland Zone, serving State Farm customers in Nebraska, Iowa, Minnesota, North Dakota, South Dakota, and Wisconsin. More than 1,300 employees staff the Lincoln Operations Center, and an additional 1,100 employees and 1,268 State Farm agents are located throughout the zone.

In the 84 years from 1922 to 2006, State Farm has grown from a small-farm mutual automobile insurer to one of the world's largest financial institutions. But despite State Farm's growth, Mecherle's original philosophy has remained: Provide insurance coverage at a fair price coupled with fair claim settlement.

State Farm's Mission, Vision, and Shared Values

State Farm's mission is to help people manage the risks of every-day life, recover from the unexpected, and realize their dreams.

We are people who make it our business to be like a good neighbor; who built a premier company by selling and keeping promises through our marketing partnership; who bring diverse talents and experiences to our work of serving the State Farm customer.

Our success is built on a foundation of shared values—quality service and relationships, mutual trust, integrity, and financial strength.

Our vision for the future is to be the customer's first and best choice in the products and services we provide. We will continue to be the leader in the insurance industry, and we will become a leader in the financial services arena. Our customers' needs will determine our path. Our values will guide us.

Products

State Farm is the number one insurer of automobiles and homes in the United States by policies in force—and has been for decades. Today, one out of five cars and homes in this country is insured by State Farm. But State Farm provides much more than automobile and home insurance.

Through more than 15 affiliated companies, State Farm provides property and casualty insurance, life and health insurance, annuities, mutual funds, and banking products.

- The State Farm Group ranked seventh in paid-for volume for ordinary life insurance among all companies in 2003.
- In just six years, State Farm Bank® has grown to become one of the country's 100 largest thrift institutions by deposits and assets.
- State Farm variable products have more than $1 billion in assets under management.
- State Farm Mutual Funds® has $6.6 billion in assets under management.
- Based on premiums written in the United States in 2005, State Farm ranks 13th among all companies selling individual health insurance.

Service

State Farm employees and agents are known as "Good Neighbors" for good reason. Whether dealing with a "fender bender" or the devastation of a midwestern tornado, State Farm's compassionate and dedicated associates help people through the emotions and turmoil of their loss.

Almost half of State Farm's employees deal in some way with claims, achieving levels of customer satisfaction that are among the highest in the industry.

Financial Strength

Financial protection for loved ones means selecting a company that has the financial strength to keep its promise to policyholders: To provide quality products and dependable service. That is why people can trust State Farm for insurance needs today and tomorrow.

State Farm has consistently received high ratings for financial strength and claims-paying ability from various independent rating agencies.

Good Citizenship

State Farm is deeply committed to good citizenship. It considers that strong, safe communities and effective schools benefit everyone, and State Farm agents and employees volunteer countless hours to support nonprofit and community-based organizations. Complementing associates' efforts, State Farm maintains charitable-giving programs, helping to build great communities through its safety, community development, and education partnerships.

Above: State Farm associates bring diverse talents and experience to their work of serving the State Farm customer.

With a history as long as Omaha's, this private, family-owned banking company, with more than 6.6 million customers, has always stayed on top of industry trends—without ever sacrificing service to do so—and continually strives to better serve its employees, customers, and communities.

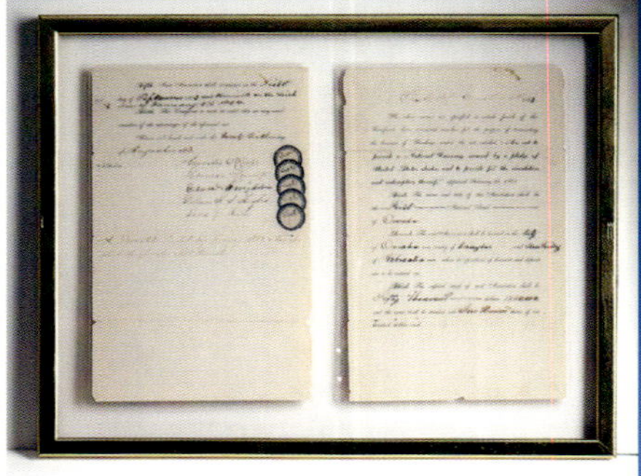

Above: First National Bank's historic charter established the firm foundation and the principles of service upon which this banking company has succeeded. Right: The tallest building in Nebraska, First National Tower, completed in 2002, graces the Omaha skyline.

Since 1857, one principle has guided First National Bank: Give customers quality products and superior service. This commitment has earned First National more than 6.6 million customers across all 50 states. Today the company employs more than 7,500 people in 35 states and manages more than $17 billion in assets. First National Tower, the bank's headquarters in downtown Omaha, symbolizes this success; at 633 feet (over 40 stories), it is the tallest building between Chicago and Denver.

Brothers Herman and Augustus Kountze opened the bank in 1857, when Omaha was barely a village; settlers had arrived just three years prior, and Nebraska had yet to attain statehood. The first Kountze Brothers bank, a small wooden building near the Missouri River, mainly trafficked in gold dust and buffalo hides.

In 1863 the bank reorganized, with well-known telegraph entrepreneur Edward Creighton as president. It applied for and received a federal charter, which made it the first national bank west of the Missouri River.

Banking on Innovation

Today, First National's holding company, First National of Nebraska, has become the largest private banking company in the United States. The bank prides itself on being family owned; Bruce Lauritzen, chairman, is the fifth generation of his family to serve First National.

Always ahead of the curve, First National issued credit cards as early as 1953. Innovation has made First National the United States' fifth-largest in-house credit card processor, seventh-largest merchant processor, 11th-largest issuer of bank cards, one of the top 20 electronic funds processors, fifth-largest agricultural bank lender (with customers in 49 states), and largest commercial-bank finance provider to the ethanol industry.

Serving Its Customers

While embracing and advancing banking technology, First National

has never lost its human touch. "As banking gets more technologically advanced, a lot of banks forget about the personal side of things," states Mark Sutko, president of Platte Valley State Bank & Trust Company in Kearney (an affiliate bank of First National). "At the end of the day, most of our business is still conducted by a person, not a computer."

First National serves the entire state, from Bloomfield (with more than 1,000 residents) to Omaha (Nebraska's largest city, with more than 500,000 residents). Whether a rancher in the Sand Hills needs an agricultural loan or a corporation needs a business expansion loan, First National helps people in all kinds and sizes of businesses, and in all types of places.

First National is also mindful that taking care of customers begins with satisfied employees. Toward this end, First National offers its employees many benefits such as flexible scheduling and a child development center (at its Omaha location), where more than 200 children of employees receive excellent child care. In fact, *Working Mother* magazine named this bank among the "100 Best Companies for Working Mothers" from 2002 to 2006.

"Our company is full of people that have been with us 10, 20, 30 years," states David Simmons, president of the Fremont National Bank and Trust Company (also an affiliated bank of First National). "We believe in a steady diet of new opportunities and new challenges. It's the best way to bring out someone's true potential."

Caring for Community

With nearly 100 Nebraska locations, First National has also earned a reputation for significant and consistent community involvement. From a $300 million investment to revive downtown Omaha to the employees who volunteer so much time and talent, First National avidly gives back.

"We're active in every community that we call home," states Rick Kolkman, president of the affiliated First National Bank in North Platte. "One, because it's the right thing to do, and two, because when a community thrives, we thrive."

Overall, this bank's corporate tenets and business practices—providing quality products and superior service, acting on a commitment to technology, and leading in community involvement—have universal appeal, which is why other states have welcomed First National Bank.

"We've got an impressive track record when it comes to growth," states Lauritzen. "We're expanding into other states and finding that people are very receptive to a bank that gives them the kind of service that other banks don't."

Above left: Platte Valley State Bank & Trust Company, located in Kearney and Grand Island, is an affiliate of First National Bank. Top right: First National built its own child development center (at its Omaha location), where more than 200 children of employees receive excellent child care. Above right: First National has been recognized for five straight years—2002 to 2006—by *Working Mother* magazine as one of the "100 Best Companies for Working Mothers" in the nation.

With fine-tuned best business practices, progressive technology, energetic people, and respect for small enterprise, this Omaha workers' compensation insurer focuses on the country's small-business market—one of the nation's largest yet underserved insurance markets—because it is often overlooked by larger insurers.

Right: Headquartered in Omaha, Nebraska, FirstComp Insurance strives to provide superior service in workers' compensation insurance for small- and medium-sized businesses nationwide. Far right: From a unique nationwide call center, FirstComp's Customer Care associates differentiate themselves from competitors as the frontline service arm of the company.

Call it the insurance company with a heart for the underdog.

FirstComp Insurance is changing the way workers' compensation insurance works, and Main Street businesses—the backbone of America's economy—are the ones that reap the benefits.

While most traditional insurers steer clear of small businesses, Omaha-based FirstComp is working for the little guy—America's plumbers, shop owners, doctors, and other entrepreneurs, who drive 95 percent of the U.S. economy.

Shaking Things Up

There were plenty of doubters in 1997 when founder and CEO Luke Yeransian and a few risk-takers set out to deliver workers' compensation insurance to the 24 million small-business owners nobody else wanted to insure—and to do it more efficiently and profitably than ever before.

"The world didn't need another insurance company when we started FirstComp," states Yeransian. "What it did need was an insurance company that was disruptive, an insurance company that was investing in new technology, new ways to service clients, and new ways to approach problems. That is what we have done at FirstComp."

Building on Success

FirstComp has broken the mold by developing best business practices that distinguish it from other carriers in an often lethargic industry. With novel approaches to workers' compensation, daring innovations, and creative insights fueling the young company, the insurance industry and America's small businesses have taken notice.

In fact, FirstComp—named one of America's 500 fastest-growing private companies for three consecutive years by *Inc.* magazine—has been one of the most profitable workers' compensation insurance companies for several years running. Rapid growth and profitability rarely go together. FirstComp achieves both through ever-expanding distribution networks and Main Street agencies, combined with paperless, Web-based technology to speed the approval process and give it one of the fastest quote turnaround times in the business.

Best Ideas, Fresh Practices

Passion . . . enthusiasm . . . energy . . . excitement are words not normally associated with an insurance company, but they aptly describe FirstComp's culture. FirstComp has stripped away many ineffective methods of traditional insurers and built a company motivated by fresh ideas and best business practices adapted from other industries. For instance, insurance underwriters learn their skills from the ground up and develop a stock-trading-floor approach to analyzing risk. Likewise, in sales, FirstComp recruits competitive, energetic, successful people from other industries and thoroughly trains its representatives in customer service and technology.

With First Comp's "people-first" philosophy, no one is holed up in a cubicle. Instead, ideas flow freely, and people explore outside-of-the-box approaches in a greenhouse of learning and development. Every team member collaborates. Innovative thinking finds open-door acceptance at every level.

Any employee can approach the president or e-mail new ideas for improving the company. This environment stimulates loyalty, responsibility, and a sense of ownership among FirstComp's teams.

"I preach to our managers what I practice myself: that you have to talk to people on the front lines who are doing the work—that's where a lot of great ideas reside," states Yeransian. "Leadership and best practices come from all levels of the organization. You have to empower people to constantly check what you're doing and come up with a better way."

Reaping the Rewards

Now in its second successful decade, FirstComp continues to flourish with its clear business strategy and its diligent best-practices management. A sales training center, a leadership development network, and community action at home and abroad will further propel the company to new heights in the future.

Ten years from now and well into the future, FirstComp Insurance Company will be doing what it has driven home from day one, according to Luke Yeransian's motto: "Stick to your knitting. Do what you're best at. Keep getting better at it than anybody else. Throw all of your heart, mind, and soul into that endeavor."

Above left: Claims Team managers John Kuehl (at left) and Todd Bertucci help oversee a team that provides superior service and expertise for both medical and lost-time claims. Adjusters conduct thorough investigations to handle each case expediently and proficiently. Above right: East Coast Region Underwriting Manager Kevin Nicotero (at right) and Underwriter Keisy Estrada are part of a team that has produced outstanding profit margins every year since the company's founding in 1997.

This successful bank with branches across the Great Plains was chartered a century ago, so it has the experience, financial stability, and maturity to fully comprehend and meet the needs of the hardworking people and businesses it serves.

Above: Great Western Bank maintains a major presence in Nebraska with locations such as this branch in the Harvey Oaks neighborhood of Omaha.

Chartered in 1907, Great Western Bank has become a key player in the Omaha metropolitan and regional business community. The bank's holding company, Omaha-based Great Western Bancorporation, is one of the largest family-owned financial institutions in the Midwest. With assets over $3 billion and 84 locations in Nebraska, South Dakota, Iowa, Missouri, and Kansas, Great Western Bancorporation is among the top five banking companies in the region. Great Western Bank serves more than 50 midwestern communities, including Omaha, Kansas City, Des Moines, Sioux Falls, and Rapid City.

At heart—and in practice—Great Western Bank remains true to its roots, when it consisted of a single bank: the Douglas County Bank in Omaha. Although much has changed in the banking industry, Great Western's operating principles have not. Now, as then, operating decisions are made locally. Great Western Bank has also been a pioneer in banking technology. In 1998 it established Bank by Mouse[SM], the first transactional Internet banking site in Nebraska. Soon after, it introduced check imaging, replacing original paper check documents with electronic copies. Today, customers use Internet banking as often as they use the bank's convenient drive-up service. In 2001, Great Western Bank opened its first branch with two-way video teller monitors, which maintain personal service for drive-up customers while increasing efficiency.

Great Western Bank retains a personal touch. For example, live telephone operators still answer calls. The bank considers that giving customers the

Deryl F. Hamann
Chairman, Great Western Bank

Dan Hamann
President, Great Western Bancorporation

Dan Brabec
President, Great Western Bank, Omaha

choice of dealing with a real person is the key to providing outstanding service and to establishing valued long-term relationships.

The bank has grown community by community, through acquiring banks and opening branches. In 2000, Great Western Bank opened its first branch inside a Wal-Mart SuperCenter in Bellevue, Nebraska. It now has five such branches throughout Omaha and five more regionally. Since acquiring the Bank of Bellevue in 1992, Great Western Bank has served military personnel with two banks at Offutt Air Force Base. Great Western Bank also serves Atkinson and O'Neill in northern Nebraska.

One of Great Western Bank's key strengths is in commercial lending. Being the lender of choice for companies in many industries, it was designated a Preferred Lender by the U.S. Small Business Administration in 1994.

Great Western Bank also provides full personal banking services; flexible lending, deposit, and investment products to help people manage their funds efficiently; trust services and private banking for those seeking to expand and manage their wealth; and in-house investment management for personal, corporate, and institutional clients.

In 2006, Deryl F. Hamann and his family celebrated 35 years of building Great Western Bancorporation into a leading regional bank holding company. Hamann is board chairman of the holding company and Great Western Bank. Dan Hamann, his son, is president of Great Western Bancorporation, and Dan Brabec, his son-in-law, is regional president of Great Western Bank, Omaha.

The leaders of Great Western Bank take pride in giving back to the communities they serve. "We think it's essential that our bankers be leaders in their communities," says Dan Hamann. Great Western Bank's employees engage in a wide variety of community service, volunteering for and contributing to numerous charitable, civic, and nonprofit groups.

Years of banking expertise and understanding the region's business needs enable Great Western Bank to offer some of the best financial products to its customers. "We're proud of the relationships we have developed, and we look forward to playing a significant role in the region's growth for many years to come," says Dan Hamann.

Assurity Security Group Inc. (ASGI)

A consolidation of the strength and stability of three well-recognized Lincoln, Nebraska–based companies, each with a century-long history, this innovative financial services firm integrates a wide range of products, services, and know-how.

Assurity Security Group Inc. (ASGI), located in Lincoln, Nebraska, is a holding company formed in 2005 by combining Assurity Life Insurance Company (above), Security Financial Life Insurance Company (top right), and Assurity Direct. In 2007, the three operating companies united as Assurity Life Insurance Company.

The formation of the holding company Assurity Security Group Inc. (ASGI) in 2005 was a landmark event that brought together three century-old Nebraska insurance companies—Assurity Life Insurance Company, Security Financial Life Insurance Company, and Lincoln Direct Life Insurance Company (later Assurity Direct)—whose values, purpose, and time-honored traditions are deeply rooted in the Great Plains.

"These longtime Lincoln-based companies share a legacy of integrity, financial strength, and the common purpose of serving the needs of Middle America," says ASGI president and CEO Tom Henning, CLU, ChFC, CFA. "With the creation of ASGI, we are building on those foundations and moving toward an exciting vision as an independent, growing, and high-performing organization."

In January 2007, the three operating companies furthered their commitment to the future by unifying under ASGI as Assurity Life Insurance Company.

Assurity Life remains dedicated to the mission that guided its founders: to help people through difficult times. Throughout its history, it has withstood many tests, never failing to honor its commitments to policyholders—not only in times of prosperity but also amid volatile markets, recessions, world wars, and the Great Depression.

"Because of the combined strengths of our joined companies, Assurity Life constitutes one of the more innovative and diversified financial services firms in our country today," Henning says. "Through our experiences with varied products and marketing strategies, our partnerships complement one another, sparking synergies that enhance a common focus—addressing the underserved needs of middle-income America and small-business clients."

Integrating multiple approaches to the marketplace, Assurity Life offers a diverse line of individual life insurance products and annuities, as well as disability and critical-illness insurance, work site products, group life insurance, pension investment management and administration, and specialty niche products designed for small businesses.

The company's combined assets in 2005 exceeded $2 billion with nearly $240 million in capital. There are some 450 associates employed locally and more than 20,000 in sales and support across the United States.

Assurity Life's long-standing community involvement, including support of artistic, cultural, and human services causes, underscores its philosophy of caring for individuals and families and maintaining quality of life for all.

Since the time of the original operating companies' founders, much has changed. Today, the successors of those visionary individuals look far beyond local and regional boundaries, but they will never lose sight of the founders' mission of helping people through difficult times.

A pioneer in processing transactions and transferring money worldwide—moving $1 trillion each year—this company has a mission: process every electronic payment worldwide from the point of sale to the point of settlement; perpetually improve e-commerce; and raise Nebraska's high-technology literacy.

Every year, First Data Corporation helps financial institutions, merchants, and consumers process more than $1 trillion in transactions. Processing credit card transactions and expediting sales (at the counter or online), First Data's more than 29,000 employees make it easy for businesses to operate and consumers to buy.

Though not a household name, First Data touches many lives. Every time someone uses a debit or credit card, visits an ATM, purchases a gift card, or writes a check, there is a good chance that First Data is behind the scenes, making the transaction possible.

First Data started in Omaha, Nebraska, in 1971 as a small company providing card-processing services to seven banks in the Midwest. First Data Resources, as it was called, became First Data Corporation, of Denver, Colorado, and made a name for itself as the world's leading credit card transaction processor. In 1976, First Data Resources processed the first Visa and MasterCard transactions. By 1980, it had 2,000 Omaha employees and annual revenues of $50 million. Today, approximately 5,000 employees worldwide, the majority of whom reside in Nebraska, work for First Data Resources, a business unit of First Data Corporation (NYSE: FDC). A major force in e-commerce, First Data serves more than 1,900 banks and other card issuers—over 601 million card accounts worldwide.

Other First Data Corporation units that operate in Nebraska offer merchant acquiring transaction processing and service, interactive voice response systems, and voice center services.

To attract leading financial companies, First Data's Omaha operations use advanced technology. Its Data Center, which operates around the clock, handles credit and debit transactions from around the world. Business continuity is one of First Data's greatest points of differentiation from its competitors. The company has one of the industry's paramount disaster-recovery systems. And First Data prints and mails millions of statements daily from its award-winning operations in Omaha.

To advance technology statewide, First Data works with Nebraska K–12 teachers, colleges, and universities. In 1996, it bought 140 acres in Omaha and donated 70 acres to the University of Nebraska's Peter Kiewit Institute of Information Science, Technology, and Engineering. This, along with First Data's educational partnerships, helps Nebraska cultivate its own world-class technology workforce.

As real-time Internet commerce accelerates, so does the need for processing, protecting, and collecting transaction data. With its partners, technology, and strategies, First Data meets those needs. Thanks to First Data innovation, consumers can apply for and receive credit in under 60 seconds to purchase books, theater tickets, and much more online. First Data continues to hasten the shift from paper to electronic transactions, driving developments and applications that make paying online fast and easy.

Since 1971, First Data's success, and that of its clients, has been linked to the resources of Nebraska.

Above: For decades, First Data has offered innovative product solutions to help merchants and financial institutions process transactions, improve cash flow, and better manage risk. Through its card issuing solutions sector, First Data allows clients to customize credit cards for their customers and label cards with the company brand, or issue signature and PIN-secured debit cards.

For more than seven decades, Pinnacle Bank—providing 'Banking, The Way Banking Should Be'—has succeeded on its philosophy and practice of honesty and hard work, doing business with a smile, and extending personal attention and common courtesy to each and every customer.

Above left: The modern facilities, comprehensive financial services, and state-of-the-art banking technologies of Pinnacle Bank are founded on a long-standing legacy of honesty, integrity, and courtesy. Above right: Roy Dinsdale serves as chairman of the board of this leading family-owned and family-operated financial institution.

The philosophy that has guided Pinnacle Bank since its founding is that a bank should be judged by what it deposits back into the community. According to this philosophy and by other measures, Pinnacle Bank is judged a success on all accounts by its clients and the communities that it serves.

Pinnacle Bank was established some 70 years ago in Palmer, Nebraska, simply because the town needed a bank.

In 1935, George Dinsdale, the patriarch of the Dinsdale family, gathered together enough money to open a bank. Dinsdale did this not because he wanted to be a banker—it wasn't exactly the normal career path for a farmer, feedlot owner, and grain storage businessman—but because the community needed a bank.

Today, Dinsdale's same down-to-earth way of thinking and doing business—including caring for and taking care of people and communities—remains at the heart of everything that Pinnacle Bank does, every day. And that's not the only legacy that George Dinsdale handed down. He also established the bank's basic tenets of hard work, honesty, and treating your neighbor like your neighbor. Roy Dinsdale, who serves as Pinnacle Bank's chairman of the board, continues George Dinsdale's legacy today.

While the modern-day employees of Pinnacle Bank may not be putting on their overalls for a day's work at the bank, they're still rolling up their sleeves and working just as hard and just as passionately as their founder did back in 1935. And they're still giving back to the communities they serve.

In fact, to ensure that this bank does not lose sight of its mission and local focus as it continues to grow, Sid Dinsdale, who serves as president of Pinnacle Bancorp, makes sure that all of the more than 95 branches are led by managers who have significant autonomy when it comes to bank operations. Every year, these managers and their employees support the communities in which they are proud to live and serve by sponsoring school activities, special events, rodeos, children's programs, and hundreds of other significant causes. This level of community involvement is just one aspect that sets Pinnacle Bank apart from other banks.

To better financially serve its communities across Nebraska, Pinnacle Bank has opened more than 45 branches statewide. These branches offer comprehensive financial services to individuals and commercial businesses to help ensure that the quality of life and of enterprise can flourish throughout Nebraska.

Furthermore, Pinnacle Bank continually invests in technologies that make banking more convenient for all its customers. And as this company's financial strength grows, its unparalleled banking products are expanded to meet the changing needs of Nebraskans. Overall, the stability of this leading financial institution is a credit to the dedication of the Dinsdales and their professional, personable employees.

This Nebraska-headquartered company—guided by 'A History of Strength. A Future of Opportunity.'—offers individuals, families, and businesses an array of insurance and financial products and services that are backed by traditional values, high ethical standards, and trusted relationships.

In 1887, there were no local life insurance companies in Lincoln, Nebraska. Most Nebraskans, if they were insured at all, used out-of-state carriers. Five businessmen saw an opportunity for a company that could provide better service to policyholders and keep money in the community. On April 6, 1887, they formed Old Line Bankers Life Insurance Company of Nebraska.

During the next century the Bankers Life Nebraska expanded to serve customers nationwide. In 1988, the company changed its name to Ameritas Life Insurance Corp.—a more accurate reflection of a national company with Midwestern roots. A decade later Ameritas Life adopted a mutual holding company corporate structure and joined forces with Acacia Life Insurance Company to form The Ameritas Acacia Companies.

On January 1, 2006, Ameritas and Acacia partnered with The Union Central Life Company to establish the UNIFI Mutual Holding Company. Operating as the UNIFI Companies,

the mutual holding company is domiciled in Nebraska and headquartered in Lincoln.

Today, Ameritas Life, Acacia Life, Union Central Life, and their affiliated companies offer a wide range of insurance and financial products and services to individuals, families, and businesses. These services include: life insurance, annuities, individual disability income insurance, group dental and eye care insurance, investments, retirement plans, banking, work site benefits, and public finance.

Ameritas' financial strength and stability are reflected in strong ratings from leading independent rating agencies such as Standard and Poor's and A. M. Best Company. Ameritas is a company built on traditional values, high ethical standards, and trusted relationships.

Ameritas is driven by a single focus—"keeping the promises we make." Ask any Ameritas associate and they will tell you that their future lies not only in taking care of their customers today, but in 50 or more years when life insurance proceeds or invested assets will be needed. That's why the promises of stability, integrity, and service are made to every customer—every day.

Both photos: For nearly 50 years, this facility has served as the headquarters for Ameritas Life Insurance Corp., formerly Bankers Life Nebraska. After a significant renovation in 2006, this building was rededicated "in the spirit of loyal customers, dedicated producers, outstanding associates—and to the promises we make to all of them."

Blue Cross and Blue Shield of Nebraska

Whether for an individual, a small local business with five employees, or a national corporation with hundreds of workers in multiple locations, Blue Cross and Blue Shield of Nebraska has the solutions for today's health care consumers.

BlueCross BlueShield of Nebraska

An Independent Licensee of the Blue Cross and Blue Shield Association.

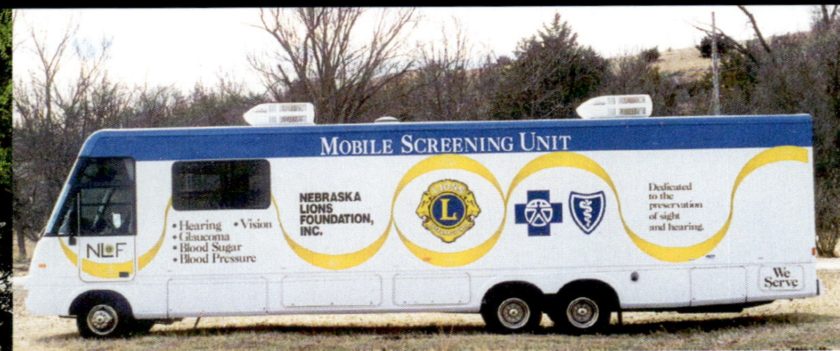

Above left: Blue Cross and Blue Shield of Nebraska is headquartered in Omaha. Above right: The popular Blue Cross and Blue Shield of Nebraska/Lions Foundation Mobile Screening Unit has provided service for more than 205,000 Nebraskans since 1989.

Providing the health and wellness solutions today's consumers want and can afford—that is the mission of Blue Cross and Blue Shield of Nebraska. Founded more than 65 years ago, it continues to offer a variety of health insurance plans for both individuals and employer group customers.

Individual plans for Nebraskans over age 65 include Medicare Supplements, Medicare Advantage PPO plans, and Medicare Part D prescription drug plans. Health care coverage options for Nebraskans under age 65 include PPO, temporary benefit plans, and limited benefit plans. Nebraska employers can choose from a number of plans and benefit options tailored to their specific requirements.

In recent years the company has introduced HSA (health savings account)-eligible, high-deductible plans, among other consumer-driven options, and group plans designed for small businesses with two to 50 employees.

Regardless of the product or service, Blue Cross and Blue Shield of Nebraska is committed to providing the best quality customer service and fast, accurate claims processing. Additionally, all Blue Cross and Blue Shield of Nebraska members have the security of knowing that they have access to the state's largest provider network, including 100 percent of nongovernmental acute care hospitals and 93 percent of physicians.

As a Nebraska-based business and employer, Blue Cross and Blue Shield of Nebraska has long been active in the communities in which its customers and employees live and work. Each year, in fact, the company funds hundreds of charitable organizations and programs in cities and towns across the state.

The Blue Cross and Blue Shield of Nebraska/Lions Foundation Mobile Screening Unit is one of the most popular and recognizable contributions the company supports each year. Since 1989, this joint effort has served more than 205,000 Nebraskans, screening them for glaucoma, visual acuity, diabetes, hypertension, and hearing problems. In fact, nearly 19,000 Nebraskans were screened in 2005 alone.

Blue Cross and Blue Shield of Nebraska, an independent licensee of the Blue Cross and Blue Shield Association, insures or provides benefit administration to more than 560,000 people. The company is committed to providing the health and wellness solutions people value most.

1%

PROFILES OF COMPANIES AND ORGANIZATIONS

Health Care, Medical Devices, Pharmaceuticals, Biotechnology

As 'Specialists in Community Service,' this JCAHO-accredited Nebraska provider of behavioral health services uses compassion and individualized treatment plans to improve the lives of emotionally troubled children and families and help adolescents and adults overcome eating disorders.

Above: Leading OMNI Behavioral Health are, from left, Morgan Kelly, J.D., M.A., treasurer and general counsel; Kendal Osbahr, M.A., director of foster care; and William Reay, Ph.D., president and CEO.

OMNI Behavioral Health, a nonprofit community-integrated behavioral health organization founded in Omaha in 1993, is devoted to providing behavioral health care to children and their families throughout Nebraska and to restoring health and dignity to individuals with eating disorders. OMNI is dedicated to using empirically based treatments to promote behaviors that enhance the individual's personal autonomy and community success. Its clinical services are provided in an Eating Disorder Clinic, Group Home Care, Foster Care, or in the family home.

Accredited by the Joint Commission on Accreditation of Healthcare Organizations (JCAHO), OMNI is also a member of the Child Welfare League of America (CWLA)—the oldest and largest membership-based organization in the nation devoted entirely to the well-being of vulnerable children.

OMNI's philosophy of treatment is based on the following principles:

- The dignity and individual rights of all persons receiving services shall be respected and protected;
- Clients are entitled to effective and efficient services in the least restrictive environment possible;
- Successful community-based treatment depends upon the active involvement of OMNI staff, clients, family, and the community;
- Clients are entitled to receive quality services that are individually designed to meet their needs.

Eating Disorder Clinic

The mission of the OMNI Eating Disorder Clinic is to provide comprehensive, individualized evaluation and treatment that is coordinated with the client's own primary care physician. The clinic is known for being located in the community instead of deep within a large medical institution and is one of only a few in the area offering a comprehensive, multidisciplinary approach to treatment.

OMNI's unique approach to treatment emphasizes the functional aspect of behavior. It is focused on all facets of the individual and on incorporating clients' natural support systems in helping them reach their goals. Treatment is available for adolescents and adult females and males. The clinic also works with individuals who wish to maintain their weight or weight-loss regimen.

Group Homes and Family Support

OMNI Group Homes and Family Support Centers are located in Beatrice, Omaha, Columbus, and Seward, Nebraska. The organization provides Group Home Care for youths who require more supervision than is customary in the foster care setting. The program strives to promote feelings of comfort, safety, and good will in the child for his or her parents, siblings, peers, and other persons involved in the child's care.

The purpose of the group home is to provide a stimulating and positive

environment in which the child is taught how to be aware of, and in control of, his or her emotions and behaviors. This is accomplished through pre-planned and systematically applied cognitive-behavior modification techniques to help the child develop skills needed for daily life and community living. Examples of these skills are positive social interaction, appropriate problem-solving, academic success, proper recreation, personal survival, and independent living.

Parents are taught the same techniques that have proven successful in shaping more adaptive behaviors with their child. This partnership with parents allows for the child's improved behavior to be transferred into the home environment. In order to maximize the child's success at home and in the community after services are completed, treatment is carried out in an environment that most reflects where and how the child will live upon leaving the group home.

Foster Care and In-Home Services

Foster Care is provided for children who have been removed from their homes but do not need the intensive supervision of a group home. It is designed to mirror a traditional family environment as closely as possible to ease the child's transition home. When siblings are removed from home, every effort is made to keep them together in the same foster home. The program's focus is on permanency and individualized treatment, with a strong preference for reunification with the family. The goal of foster care is to achieve stability, safety, and a sense of permanence for each child; to develop positive, supportive relationships in each family; and to pursue adoption if a child is unable to return home.

Because early intervention often helps families stay together while working on behavior change, OMNI offers both Home-Based Therapy and Intensive Family Preservation Services to families with mental health or delinquency problems. The goal is to eliminate the need for children's removal from home by providing intensive, timely, and individualized services in the home.

By providing treatment and support for individuals and families with emotional and behavioral issues, OMNI helps people find hope and dignity, achieve their full potential, and gain greater control over their future. The organization will continue to improve the lives of children and adults throughout Nebraska with its culture of compassion and self respect and its commitment to empirically based, individualized treatments.

Above: OMNI provides Group Home Care (left), believing that even if children must be separated from their family, they should not be separated from their community (right).

Pfizer Inc's Lincoln, Nebraska, production facility—the largest manufacturing site within Pfizer dedicated to the production of animal health products—is one of the world's most advanced technological centers for large-scale production of vaccines; its products are exported to more than 60 countries.

Above: Pfizer Inc's manufacturing plant in Lincoln, Nebraska, located at 601 West Cornhusker Highway, covers more than 145 acres. Right: In the mechanical room of Pfizer's freeze-drying facility, a maintenance technician conducts a routine preventive-maintenance check on a freeze dryer to ensure the utmost efficiency in equipment performance.

Pfizer Inc's manufacturing plant in Lincoln, Nebraska, has long served as the company's center for the production of animal health biologicals and pharmaceuticals. The Lincoln operation is emerging as a center of excellence for animal health biologicals and will, ultimately, focus entirely on the high quality manufacture of animal health vaccines. The Lincoln organization is part of Pfizer Global Manufacturing, a network of more than 60 manufacturing sites in more than 25 countries and a strategic asset to Pfizer, the world leader in human and animal health medicines.

The site's global presence has its roots in the early-20th-century birth of the animal health industry. Pfizer's Lincoln site has grown dramatically not only in physical size but also in global impact.

It was 1919 when Dr. Carl J. Norden Sr., a young immigrant from Sweden, fulfilled his dream of starting an ethical drug firm and selling its products to veterinarians. His company, known as Norden Laboratories, enjoyed steady growth through its first 40 years, first by distributing products made by others and then by discovering, developing, and producing its own biological and pharmaceutical products for livestock.

In 1959 Norden Laboratories became a subsidiary of Philadelphia-based SmithKline & French Laboratories. At that time, Norden Laboratories was marketing approximately 60 biological and 165 pharmaceutical products. The merger provided the philosophical and financial resources for the organization to grow and thrive. The next three decades were an impressive period of growth for Norden Laboratories, in which many new products for both livestock and companion animals were introduced.

In July 1989 SmithKline Beckman (formerly SmithKline & French) merged with Beecham Group and the once fully autonomous Norden Laboratories became an operating unit. The facility was designated as the worldwide manufacturing center for all SmithKline Beecham Animal Health biological products and was chartered with the production of additional pharmaceutical products.

In 1994 a state-of-the-art plant for manufacture of bulk biological antigens for vaccine production was completed and dedicated. Later that same year, the entire SmithKline Beecham Animal Health business was purchased by Pfizer.

Pfizer, founded in 1849, is dedicated to better health and greater access to health care for people and their valued animals. More than 100,000 Pfizer colleagues worldwide work for a healthier world through the discovery and development of innovative medicines, the manufacture of high quality products, and global leadership in corporate responsibility.

Today the 145-acre Pfizer Lincoln property in northwest Lincoln, with manufacturing facilities of more than 920,000 square feet, serves as a global manufacturing center for bulk biological antigens for livestock and companion animal vaccines, as well as biological-product finishing and packaging operations for vaccines.

Pharmaceutical products are regulated by the FDA and international regulatory agencies. Production in Lincoln includes anti-infectives, parasiticides, liquid and tablet nutritional supplements, and anthelmintic pastes and suspensions.

Biological products are regulated by the USDA and international regulatory agencies. Annual production at the Lincoln plant exceeds 650 million vaccine doses. Major biological products made at Pfizer Lincoln are: RespiSure®, BovShield®, FarrowSure®, and the Vanguard® product line.

Biologicals are key to Pfizer's global animal health business. To support the expected launch of new biological products in late stage development, as well as the anticipated sales growth of existing products, two significant expansions have taken place at the Pfizer Lincoln facility since 2004. The first project included the installation of new freeze-drying equipment used to manufacture vaccines, accomplished by the conversion of existing warehouse space into a new production area. The second project was the construction of a new veterinary medicine biologicals pilot plant for the transfer of biologicals from research and development into manufacturing.

The multimillion-dollar capital investments in Pfizer's Lincoln facility contribute to its technological excellence, but the true strength of the operation is the organization's employees, who are a testament to the organization's scientific expertise and dedication to continuous improvement and the "Right First Time" strategy for performance.

Pfizer Lincoln employees are also engaged in the community, taking an active role, as an organization and as individuals, in making the community in which they work and live a better place. Pfizer Lincoln has been among the largest contributors to the Lincoln Lancaster County United Way campaign for several years. Pfizer is also a strong supporter of math and science education, environmental protection programs, and cultural activities.

Pfizer Lincoln is committed to "Working for a Healthier World™."

Above left: The process of filling and capping single-dose vaccine vials is fully automated in Pfizer's newest biologicals production unit. Here, 16 vials are filled simultaneously. Above right: Pfizer Lincoln's Pilot Lab is dedicated to the scale-up of new products that come to manufacturing from research and development. Here, in the bacterial suite, technicians are scaling up bacterins from a 30-liter fermentor to a 1,000-liter vessel and, then, moving the antigen into a continuous-flow centrifuge.

With a reputation for excellence, innovation, and extraordinary patient care, this not-for-profit teaching hospital is regionally and nationally recognized for its oncology, neurology, and cardiology programs, as well as its organ and bone marrow transplant programs.

Above: The Nebraska Medical Center is a respected leader in cardiology, neurology, oncology, and solid organ transplantation.

The Nebraska Medical Center of Omaha, Nebraska, belongs to an elite class of American hospitals. In 2005 J. D. Power and Associates recognized The Nebraska Medical Center for providing an "outstanding patient experience" and named it a Distinguished Hospital for Service Excellence. Only 20 percent of U.S. hospitals achieve this distinction, and The Nebraska Medical Center is Nebraska's first.

"We have worked diligently to assemble such an astounding, well-rounded medical team," says president and CEO Glenn Fosdick, Fellow of the American College of Healthcare Executives (FACHE). "The wide spectrum of talent present in our physicians, nursing staff, and technicians guarantees that patients of all ages and illnesses will receive the best care possible. We are proud to offer such a high level of excellence."

History of Growth

Today the 689-bed acute-care facility is the main teaching hospital for the University of Nebraska Medical Center (UNMC), but it dates back to 1869 when Nebraska's first hospital, Clarkson Hospital (then called Good Samaritan), opened. In 1917 the University of Nebraska Medical School opened University Hospital in Omaha. Not until 1997 did University Hospital and Clarkson Regional Health System merge to become the Nebraska Health System. Before the merger, Clarkson and University Hospital dominated Nebraska's record of medical milestones. In 2003 the name was changed to The Nebraska Medical Center.

Specialty Medical Services

Dedicated to compassionate, quality patient care, The Nebraska Medical Center also delivers excellent specialized medicine. A recognized leader in organ and bone marrow transplants, oncology, neurology, and cardiology, The Nebraska Medical Center staffs 950 physicians covering all specialties. In 2005, 176 of them, culled from 34 specialties, were named to the national Best Doctors in America list.

In the area of neurological sciences, The Nebraska Medical Center provides some of the most advanced technological treatments available. Strokes are the leading cause of disability in U.S. adults, claiming some 750,000 victims annually. The Nebraska Medical Center Stroke Center is dedicated to preventing and treating strokes. Certified by the Joint Commission on Accreditation of Healthcare Organizations (JCAHO), it is the only nationally certified stroke center in the state. The stroke team at The Nebraska Medical Center is poised to treat patients as soon as possible after the initial onset of stroke symptoms.

The Nebraska Medical Center's Epilepsy Center provides new treatments and hope for people with epilepsy. The center uses a four-phase monitoring and treatment program with highly advanced diagnostic equipment.

The Nebraska Medical Center Organ Transplant Program, one of the

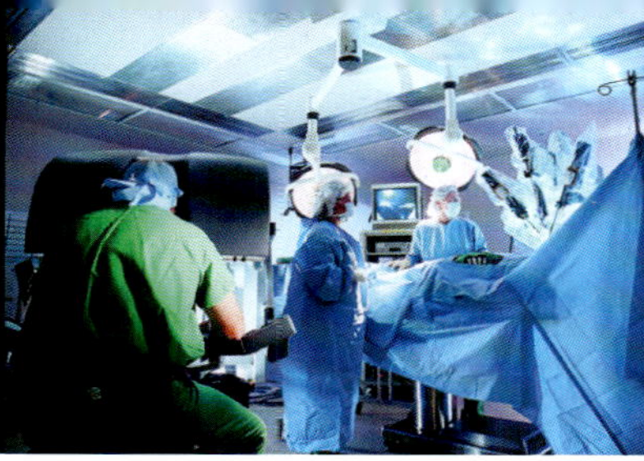

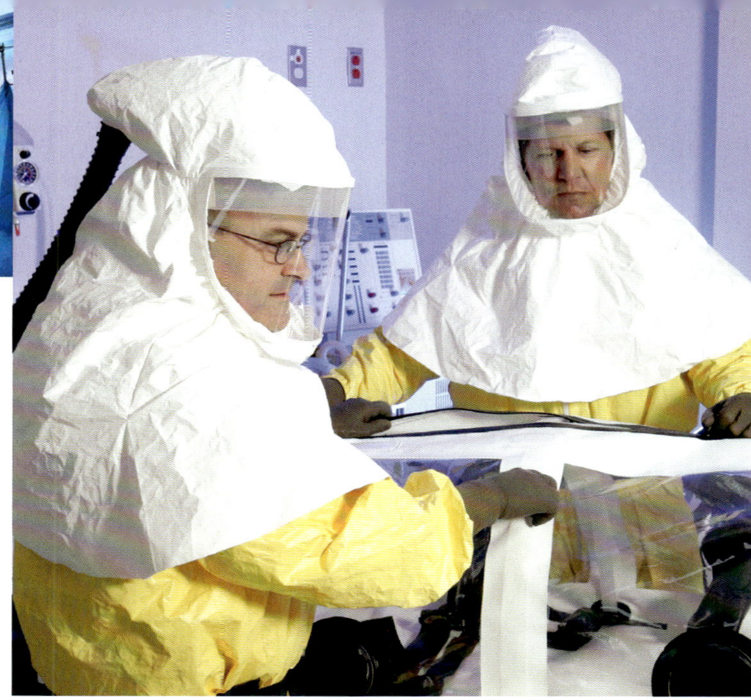

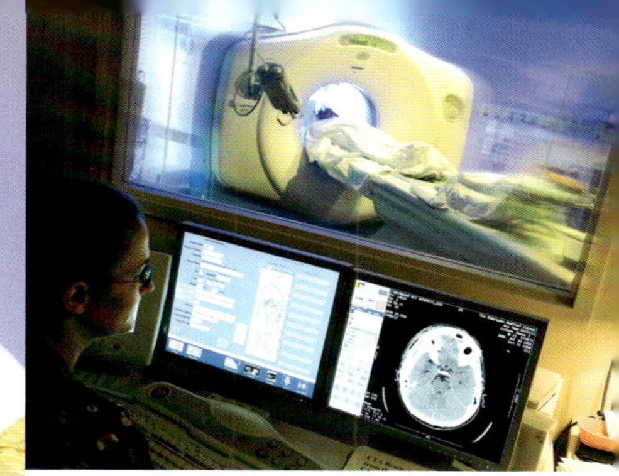

country's most active and reputable, helps patients with diseases of the liver, small intestine, kidneys, pancreas, heart, and lungs. The Lied Transplant Center, which opened in 1999, is a national model in the care for solid organ and cancer-related transplant patients. It lets doctors and researchers develop optimal practice and care methods for transplant patients. The facility houses a 24-hour clinic, research laboratories, and suites for patients and families. The transplant center uses a unique cooperative care approach to help the patient transition from hospital to home.

The Nebraska Medical Center also has one of the most respected and advanced cancer care departments in the country. Staffed by leading cancer specialists, the center is one of few in the United States to offer ultrasound-based radiation for treating prostate cancer. The Nebraska Medical Center is also the only hospital in the state with intensity-modulated radiation therapy (IMRT), a powerful technology that improves radiation targeting of tumors without damaging surrounding healthy tissue.

Cardiovascular disease being the number one killer in the country, The Nebraska Medical Center offers a continuum of personal, patient-centered heart care services spanning cardiac rehabilitation and stress tests to brachytherapy, open-heart surgery, and more.

The Nebraska Medical Center also has the largest biocontainment unit in the country. The 10-bed unit is used for handling highly contagious and deadly diseases. The Nebraska Medical Center, UNMC, and Nebraska Health and Human Services System work together to run the unit, which, Fosdick says, "allows us the opportunity to help hospitals across the country care for patients who come into contact with deadly, highly contagious diseases" such as smallpox, avian flu, or multidrug-resistant tuberculosis.

Healthy Prognosis for the Future

In 2006 The Nebraska Medical Center announced plans for a state-of-the-art complex in Bellevue, Nebraska. The Bellevue Medical Center will encompass 200,000 square feet for comprehensive patient services, including emergency care, obstetrics, inpatient and outpatient surgery, intensive care, cardiac catheterization, radiology, lab testing, and a pharmacy. A 60,000-square-foot medical building will adjoin the main hospital. The campus is scheduled to open in 2008.

Fosdick says, "Bellevue Medical Center will provide a natural extension of the extraordinary care our patients have come to expect. We are very excited to be working in partnership with the Bellevue community to help meet the health care needs of this growing area."

Access to excellent health care is vital to a community's economic development and quality of life. Since 1869, The Nebraska Medical Center has proven this time and again. By remaining at the forefront of innovative medical treatments and continuing to provide extraordinary patient care and medical resources, the prognosis for a healthy future looks promising—for The Nebraska Medical Center and the community.

Above left: The Nebraska Medical Center provides a continuum of heart care services, including innovative treatments and personal, patient-centered care. Above center: The Nebraska Medical Center is home to the largest biocontainment unit in the United States. The 10-bed unit is equipped to handle highly contagious and deadly infectious conditions. Above right: The Neurological Sciences unit at The Nebraska Medical Center provides some of the most advanced treatment technologies available.

Methodist Health System and Methodist Hospital

Providing highly rated health care for people who live in eastern Nebraska and western Iowa, this health network—the first not-for-profit health care system in the region—comprises two hospitals with long traditions of compassion, as well as the facilities and professionals to serve any patient need.

Right: From cancer care, cardiology, and neurosurgery to women's services, orthopedics, and comprehensive diagnostic services, Methodist Hospital—one of two Methodist Health System hospitals—offers unparalleled care and some of the nation's most technologically advanced therapies. Omaha-area consumers consistently rank Methodist as their first choice for quality care.

Methodist Health System (MHS) was formed in 1982, but its hospitals—Methodist Hospital of Omaha, Nebraska, and Jennie Edmundson Hospital of Council Bluffs, Iowa—began shaping the area's health care environment more than 120 years ago.

The oldest not-for-profit health care system in the area, MHS employs some 5,000 people. Besides Methodist Hospital (the system's flagship facility) and the 255-bed Jennie Edmundson Hospital, MHS includes Methodist Physicians Clinic, Nebraska's largest private multispecialty group practice; Nebraska Methodist College—The Josie Harper Campus, a fully accredited health professions college; and a separate foundation for each hospital.

Methodist Hospital: A History of Caring

In 1891, members of the Methodist Episcopal Church in Omaha established a hospital at 20th and Harney streets. By providing physical care in a spiritual setting, Methodist Hospital began a tradition that still characterizes the hospital—and the whole health system—today.

In 1968 Methodist Hospital moved to its current location at 84th Street and West Dodge Road. This move was prompted by its own growth as well as Omaha's expansion westward. Today a 430-bed acute-care facility with some 800 physicians, Methodist Hospital offers a full range of educational, medical, and surgical services. Methodist Hospital is on the cutting edge of technology. It is among 2 percent of U.S. hospitals that use patient and medication bar code scanning to ensure that the right patient gets the right dose of the right medicine at the right time. It is also converting to an electronic health records system so health professionals can easily access complete patient records.

Along with these services, Methodist Hospital specializes in cardiology, neuroscience, oncology, orthopedics, urology, and women's services. It leads the area in obstetrical care, delivering more than 3,800 babies annually, and it plans to build a women's hospital at 192nd Street and West Dodge Road.

We at the Methodist Health System are proud to define the 'Meaning of Care' for the Omaha community. Our superb medical staff, working in coordination with highly skilled employees, has established a tradition of providing compassionate care while utilizing the latest medical technologies in the diagnosis and treatment of patients throughout the region.

John Fraser

Chief Executive Officer, Methodist Health System

Distinguishing Specialties and Technologies

Named for John W. Estabrook, Methodist Hospital's president from 1959 to 1992, the Methodist Estabrook Cancer Center treats more cancer patients than any other hospital in the area, providing state-of-the-art treatment. Its oncology research department assesses every patient's eligibility for national research studies using new and promising therapies. Nine percent of the cancer center's patients become trial participants, compared to the national average of 2 to 3 percent.

The center offers some of the most advanced multidisciplinary approaches and technologies in the area. Methodist Hospital has Omaha's first and only Leksell Gamma Knife®, a noninvasive machine used to aim a precise dose of radiation with absolute accuracy to destroy cancer cells, shrink tumors, or control disease progression. The center also has computer-aided detection (CAD) mammography, two linear accelerators for radiation therapy, image-guided radiation therapy (IGRT), and intensity modulated radiation therapy (IMRT).

Methodist Hospital has distinguished orthopedics and sports medicine departments as well. It is one of only 176 hospitals nationwide, and the only one in the state, to be ranked in *U.S.News & World Report*'s 2006 America's Best Hospitals Survey.

To help people beat heart disease, Methodist Hospital provides a full continuum of cardiovascular services: a state-of-the-art cardiac catheterization lab, diagnostic testing, open-heart surgery, and rehabilitation. And all day every day, the hospital's emergency department chest pain center, staffed with trained personnel and equipped with the latest diagnostic technology, rapidly evaluates patients with chest pain.

Among other firsts, Methodist Hospital is the first Nebraska hospital to attain Magnet status, in 2004. The gold standard of nursing excellence, this award is given to fewer than 2 percent of U.S. hospitals.

Works of the Heart

The Methodist Hospital Foundation funds programs in four areas: cancer care, charitable care, community service, and education. For example, the foundation helps sustain the hospital's Lung and Thoracic Oncology Clinic and, for genetic testing, the Cancer Prevention and Hereditary Cancer Risk Clinic. These centers work to prevent, diagnose, and treat cancer.

The Foundation also funds the Heidi Wilke SANE/SART (sexual assault nurse examiner/sexual assault response team) program, the only one of its kind in the Omaha area. It provides immediate, comprehensive, and compassionate care to victims of sexual assault. The foundation also supports Nebraska Methodist College—The Josie Harper Campus in Omaha, an MHS affiliate. This health professions college offers undergraduate, graduate, and certificate programs in nursing and allied health.

Backed by more than a century of caring, MHS serves its patients with skilled compassion balanced with today's technology.

Above left: Methodist Hospital is home to the Elektra Synergy® image-guided radiation therapy (IGRT) system, one of only 20 in the world. The most advanced IGRT system available, this machinery offers technology that allows doctors to see and treat tumors with ultimate accuracy, targeting radiation within fractions of a millimeter to spare healthy tissues.

Focused on the happiness and well-being of individuals, this provider of elder care services brings 'Dignity in Life' to the residents of 33 facilities in five states. Its high quality nursing homes are staffed by 2,700 dedicated team members and have earned a reputation for providing outstanding personal care.

Above left: Jack and Eldora Vetter, founders of Vetter Health Services, Inc. (VHS), have always believed that the elderly deserve to be treated with dignity and respect.

Since 1975, Jack and Eldora Vetter have been committed to the mission of "Dignity in Life"—making available places to live where senior citizens would feel respected, secure, comfortable, and happy. It is the "Vetter Way." This mission guides Vetter Health Services (VHS) and its team members in every aspect of service. From the company's home office in Omaha to its facilities in Nebraska, Kansas, Iowa, Missouri, and Wyoming, living the "Vetter Way" has made VHS an outstanding example of excellence to others in its profession.

This exceptional dedication to fulfilling the mission of "Dignity in Life," inspires the organization and its team members to meet the residents' physical, emotional, and spiritual needs. The goal is to care for individuals in a way that makes them feel respected, fulfilled, useful, healthy, and secure. This means that each facility is built around the individual needs of the residents and their community.

VHS is focused on relationships, which it believes are important to its success. By developing strong connections between people who genuinely care about each other, residents and team members become a family of healthy, happy, and productive individuals.

Satisfying work relationships also are important to the happiness of caregivers, so Vetter Health Services is committed to providing a work environment that is encouraging, positive, fulfilling, and fun for team members. VHS believes this is the best way to build a comfortable home filled with life, love, and happiness.

The Vetter Vision

Each VHS vision statement upholds its philosophy of quality and caring:

- Quality of Life is the top priority, and one of the many reasons that VHS facilities are among the most respected. Each resident deserves a life filled with happiness, comfort, and meaning, lived in a secure and healthy home where every member of the family is loved, nurtured, and encouraged to live life to the fullest.
- Quality Care is the VHS dedication to provide personalized care and services that achieve extraordinary results and exceed the expectations of those the company serves.
- Excellent Teams are created by hand-selecting staff members who embody the values VHS believes in. Team members' actions are driven by a "Yes, I Can" attitude, to listen, to be honest, and to put their heart into their service, showing that they really do care.
- Quality Reputation is achieved by building relationships of trust, confidence, and loyalty through quality services, the honesty of staff, and involvement in the community. VHS administrators and other staff members are considered to be friends, valued colleagues, and solid citizens within the community.
- Outstanding Facilities—a VHS hallmark—send a welcoming message to residents and visitors. Attractive buildings are thoughtfully designed and well maintained, enhancing the quality of life for residents and team members. Facilities are built and maintained with love and a deep sense of responsibility for the lives being served.

- Stewardship is an all-encompassing principle that includes the organization's responsible use of resources to serve residents, to ensure the long-term financial stability of the company, to reinvest in people and facilities, and to pursue growth opportunities.

The Vetter Values

The organization's values—service, integrity, teamwork, and excellence—are closely tied to its vision statements. Service is performed not out of obligation but as a labor of love, driven by the motto "Family Serving Family." For VHS, integrity means "always acting with honesty, fairness, and compassion in a way that will make God smile." Teamwork is built on mutual trust and respect, as team members seek to understand others and show their appreciation for one another. Excellence is a way of life for VHS and at its facilities. It means continually improving, exceeding expectations, and remaining committed to becoming the best of the best.

VHS and its facilities have been honored by receiving numerous industry awards, including the American Health Care Association's Quality Awards, the Edgerton Quality Awards, the State Excellence in Long-term Care Awards, and internal honors with the VHS Quality Awards.

The Vetter Foundation was formed in 1992 by Jack and Eldora Vetter as a way of showing their gratitude for having the opportunity to serve others. The twofold purpose of the foundation supports Christian organizations that serve the needy and sponsors educational opportunities to improve the quality of education in health care. The foundation's impact can be seen around the world from improving the quality and cost of elderly services in rural areas, to disaster relief efforts, to rural ministries to African villages. The Vetter Foundation is an extension of VHS's vision to serve and meet people's needs.

From its start, VHS has been committed to incorporating a deep understanding of a resident's need for dignity into its facilities. With the help and dedication of many, Vetter Health Services has become a living example of how one can give senior citizens the quality of life and quality care they deserve.

Alegent Health

This faith-based, not-for-profit health care system embraces innovations in medical and information technology, providing a continuum of care while reaching into the surrounding community to address consumer needs in treatment, cost, and choice.

Alegent Health is the largest not-for-profit, faith-based health care system in Nebraska and southwestern Iowa. With nine acute care hospitals, more than 100 sites of service, and roughly 8,500 employees and 2,500 volunteers, Alegent Health prides itself on providing high quality, patient-centered care for the body, mind, and spirit of every person. Within the Alegent Health system, patients and their families find a continuum of care, from women's and children's services, primary care, wellness counseling, and senior care to cardiovascular services, orthopaedics, oncology, physical rehabilitation, and behavioral health.

Born of the union between two premier health organizations with common core values and more than 100 years of combined experience—Catholic Health Initiatives and Immanuel Health Systems—Alegent Health's roots are deep, its branches wide.

Alegent Health has an exceptional reputation for quality that results in large part from its drive to innovate. "Alegent Health is fully aware of our greater responsibilities to seek out innovations that improve patient care and to extend our healing mission beyond our walls and into the communities we serve," says Lawrence J. Beckman, chairman of the Alegent Health Board of Directors.

Alegent Health is already recognized for its high standard of care, having attained patient satisfaction ratings in the 95th percentile. All five of its metropolitan hospitals received 5-Star Awards from Professional Research Consultants, Inc. for overall quality of inpatient care in 2005.

However, the challenge of how to define, measure, and communicate quality in a way that empowers patients to best manage their own health care remains. To better define and improve clinical quality in the long term, Alegent Health is engaged in a multitude of innovative initiatives. One of its most aggressive initiatives is its Right Track accelerated decision-making process. This process brings together stakeholders in a space constructed expressly for the purpose of dialogue, decision making, and planning. Right Track accelerated decision making will revolutionize Alegent Health's clinical service areas.

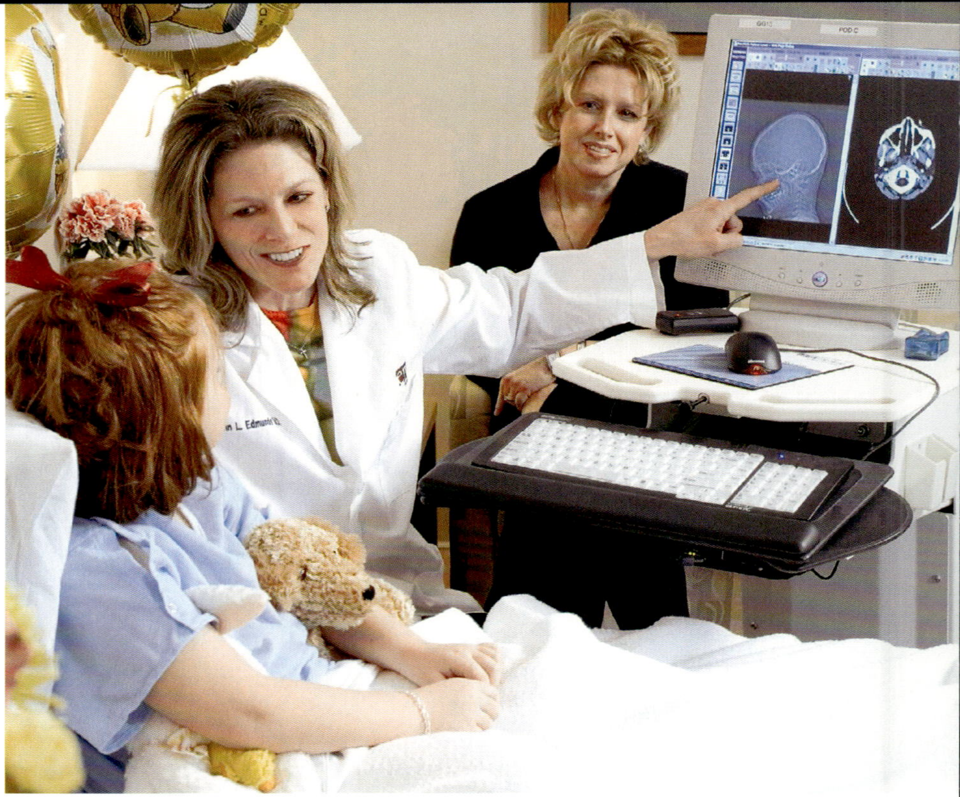

Right: Alegent Health's team of physicians, nurses, technicians, and staff complement state-of-the-art medical technologies with "state-of-the-heart" healing and health care.

Alegent Health is committed to not only being a leader in innovative ideas, but also to employing the best advances in technology—as well as innovations that improve the diagnosis, treatment,

and efficiency of quality patient care. With a significant capital investment and a strategic alliance with Siemens Medical Systems, a leader in diagnostic and clinical solutions, Alegent Health effectively merges medical technology with information technology. The outcome is everything from efficient electronic medical records to digital imaging that allows for nearly instantaneous interpretation by clinicians.

"Technology is a tool to help us provide quality care," says Ken Lawonn, senior vice president and chief information officer. "It helps the physician to harness the vast information available and bring it to bear, real-time, to improve patient care."

Alegent Health has made a commitment to positively impact the health of the citizens of Nebraska and southwest Iowa. "Our mission calls for us to address the health status of the communities we serve," Wayne Sensor, chief executive officer, explains. "This is not just limited to inpatient and outpatient services. It means that we reach into our communities and find out what the needs are for all we serve."

In the summer of 2004, Alegent Health introduced the Community Benefit Trust. The trust provides grants to community groups and nonprofit organizations that are taking innovative approaches to caring for the communities' most underserved and vulnerable populations. Between $5 million and $7 million is allocated from net patient service revenues annually to support community programs through the Alegent Health Community Benefit Trust.

As Alegent Health celebrates more than 10 successful years, it does so with the realization that change is needed in the health care industry. Sensor explains, "Too often we have built health care to suit our needs; now we need to create a system more reflective of the quality, innovation, and care consumers want."

Alegent Health strongly believes there is tremendous benefit to putting the consumer back in the driver's seat and making the link between care, cost, and consumer choice more apparent. In January 2006, Alegent Health began offering two new consumer-directed health care plans for its employees. The plans will serve as models for other area businesses.

Alegent Health is launching a new era of improvement and growth, yet one constant remains according to President Richard A. Hachten II: "We are focused on quality and innovation and we believe the current strategic plan will take us to the next level, as a world-class leader through quality and innovation. Where we are today wouldn't be possible without our passionate commitment to our mission and the tools we have to make that manifest for our employees and our patients. That will always be the foundation for our success."

Above left: Alegent Health's doctors work together to provide high standards of care, ensuring clinical quality for the present and the future. Above right: Compassionate hands-on medical and rehabilitative care has resulted in patient satisfaction ratings in the 95th percentile for Alegent Health and its dedicated staff.

Creighton University Medical Center

This highly respected academic medical center—one of the largest health care providers in Nebraska—is devoted to discovery through research, to education through training future physicians and other health care professionals, and to patient care through the delivery of new therapies to improve patients' lives.

Above left: Creighton University Medical Center (CUMC) is an academic medical center teaching tomorrow's health care professionals while striving for excellence in diagnosis and treatment today. Above right: CUMC surgeon Charles Filipi, M.D., instructs a new generation of physicians.

Since before the turn of the 20th century, physicians, teachers, and researchers have joined together at Creighton University Medical Center (CUMC) to provide the best possible medical care to patients throughout the region. Through the academic medical center's affiliation with Creighton University, one of the nation's 28 Jesuit Catholic educational institutions, these highly skilled specialists have based CUMC's comprehensive efforts on a long-standing philosophy and enduring healing mission.

"Nationally, we are one of the few hospitals that is associated with a Jesuit medical school," explains Linda Ollis, CUMC hospital CEO. "It is not just the teaching mission, it is teaching health care that is grounded in the principles of Jesuit education and service to others."

Focused on Patient Care, Research, and Teaching

At CUMC, quality patient care involves treating the whole person by staying on the leading edge of medical treatments and advancements while having access to a large network of resources. The organization includes the CUMC hospital, a 334-bed acute care facility; the Creighton University schools of medicine, nursing, dentistry, pharmacy, and health professions; Creighton Medical Laboratories; the Center for Health Policy and Ethics; and Creighton Medical Associates, a network of nearly 300 faculty physicians who practice in clinics and outreach sites throughout Nebraska and southwest Iowa. "In addition to providing exceptional care to patients," Ollis says, "we are conducting research and training future health care providers."

By combining research and teaching with patient-centered medical care, CUMC has built a national reputation in multiple fields. Today the organization's high-level cardiac program, cancer services, and specialized surgery program have gained national recognition.

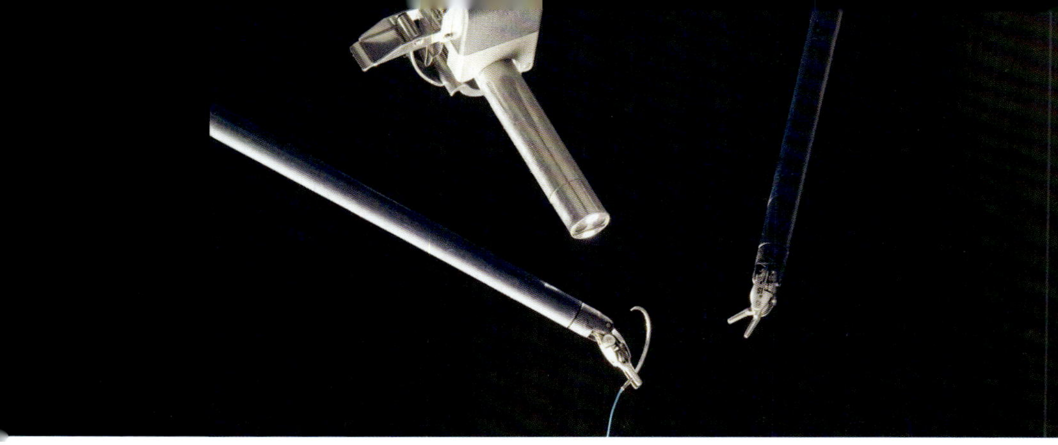

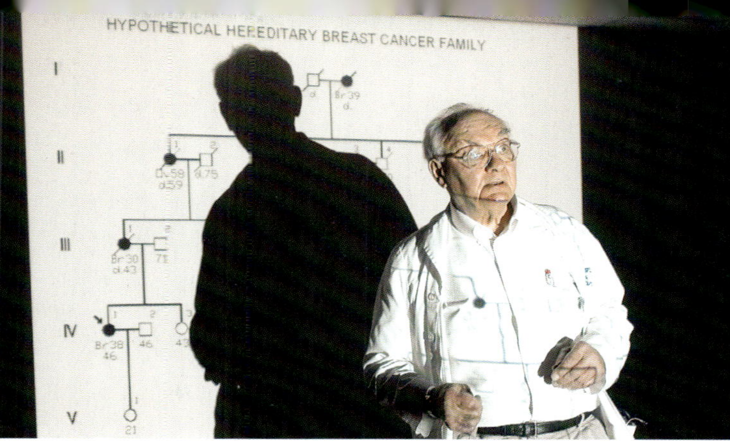

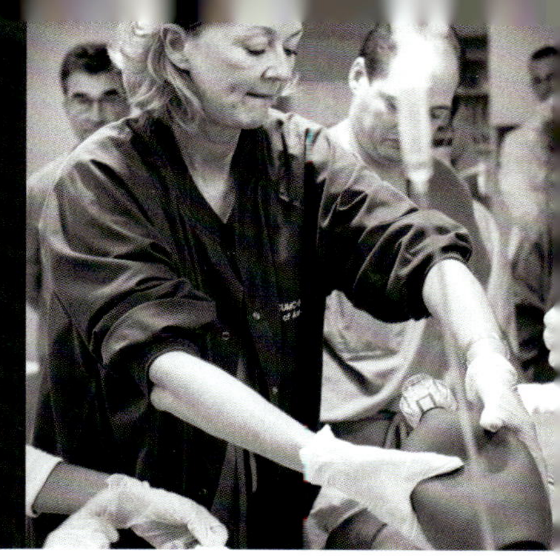

The facility is also recognized internationally for advancements in cancer, genetics, osteoporosis, and minimally invasive surgery. Solucient, a leading source of health care information, has recognized CUMC as one of the top 100 U.S. teaching hospitals.

High Honors and Awards

In 2005, the U.S. Department of Health and Human Services awarded CUMC its inaugural Medal of Honor. This is in recognition of CUMC's success in increasing organ donations in Nebraska through its partnership with the National Organ Donation Breakthrough Collaborative. CUMC is one of only 180 hospitals in the nation to earn the organization's prestigious Medal of Honor.

Also in 2005, the American Heart Association recognized CUMC for its 100 percent participation in the association's Get With The Guidelines–Coronary Artery Disease (GWTG-CAD) and Get With The Guidelines–Heart Failure (GWTG-HF) programs, designed to ensure that patients with cardiovascular disease are consistently treated and discharged with appropriate medications and instructions to minimize the risk of a second heart attack or stroke. "Creighton University Medical Center's 100 percent commitment is something we hope other health organizations will follow," states Gray Ellrodt, M.D., chairman for the association's GTWG Steering Committee.

These types of acknowledgments are a result of CUMC's pledge to provide advanced care and new therapies that pave the way for others in the medical field. "As members of a teaching hospital, our physicians and staff strive to develop new technology and serve as early implementers for new treatments," says Stephen Lanspa, M.D., senior vice president for medical affairs.

Charles Filipi, M.D., FACS, who focuses on minimally invasive surgery and its development, agrees. "There is some very important work being done here," he says. "Part of our mission is research, and the underlying core values are to advance medical science. As we have successfully operationalized our mission and core values, patients in communities near and far have benefited greatly and will continue to benefit in the future."

In areas such as specialized surgery, CUMC's physicians have been able to apply a wide range of sophisticated procedures, from esophageal laparoscopic surgeries using the robotic da Vinci® Surgery System to the Center for Breast Care's minimally invasive breast cancer treatments and same-day tissue diagnosis. The ability to study and implement these techniques has attracted some of the best specialists to CUMC as well as other physicians who want to learn from them.

One such expert is Robert Fitzgibbons Jr., M.D., FACS, a global authority on hernia repair. A member of the CUMC team, he sees firsthand how the facility works to benefit patients locally and from around the world, particularly in regards to laparoscopy. "What is important is the fact that we are doing research, in addition to the surgeries," he notes. "I hope area residents know what a great resource they have. We are more than a hospital."

Committed to the Community

The work performed at CUMC has made the medical center a valuable regional, national, and international resource—about one-third of its patients come from outside of the Omaha area. Nevertheless, the medical center's commitment to the local community remains strong. The center sponsors major community events and supports nonprofit organizations year-round. It also coordinates communication between the hospital and neighborhood clinics to provide continuity of care, and it serves as a regional trauma center.

Every day Creighton University Medical Center strives to improve the lives of people who have come to count on the center's high level of care 24 hours a day, 365 days a year. "We care for some of the region's most critically ill patients, smallest infants, and individuals with complex injuries and illnesses," Ollis says. "We are an academic medical center that brings together some of the most innovative patient care, teaching, and health care research in the region."

Above left: CUMC is one of few Nebraska hospitals to use the da Vinci® surgical robot, which inserts tiny instruments into the body through small incisions. Smaller incisions mean less scarring and recovery time. Above center: CUMC cancer specialist Henry Lynch, M.D., revolutionized cancer research, tracing the causes of many cancers to heredity. Above right: CUMC's trauma team stands ready 24 hours a day, seven days a week to treat some of the region's most complex illnesses and injuries.

Recognized across the globe as a leading innovator of products for the clinical laboratory, this Omaha-based industry pioneer develops and manufactures control products for the automated instruments used in testing. Among its many achievements, it has gained a 65 percent worldwide market share for hematology controls.

Above: Connie Ryan is president and Wayne Ryan, Ph.D., is chairman of the board and CEO of Streck, Inc., headquartered in Omaha.

A company with a facility for adapting quickly to new demands, Streck, Inc. manufactures sophisticated control products for advanced clinical laboratories that are blazing trails in hematology, immunology, and chemistry. Streck was one of the first companies to develop hematology reference controls. It also invests significant resources in research and development—in such areas as molecular biology, cell fixatives, immunology, and transport reagents—to support evolving needs.

Established in 1971 in Omaha, Streck is a pioneer in the creation of innovative laboratory controls. The company was founded by Wayne Ryan, Ph.D., today chairman of the board and CEO. Streck developed some of the first controls for automated hematology instruments—a breakthrough for hematology laboratories of the day—and hematology controls, reagents, and support products continue to be its core business. Additional product lines include flow cytometry controls and preservatives, chemistry controls, sedimentation rate products, and quality-control devices. In the 1970s Ryan was one of the relatively few scientists in the world who understood the importance of hematology quality-control products. He states, "Many of the most dramatic advances in medicine today are dependent on consistency and accuracy in the clinical laboratory, and we at Streck are committed to providing products to assure that consistency and accuracy." This mission is guided by the founder's daughter Connie Ryan, who heads the company as president, and it is implemented by Streck's 300-plus dedicated employees. Working together, they have garnered more than 40 patents for the company. Streck's 200,000-square-foot facility is designed to support the work of world-class biochemists and technicians.

Streck's products are manufactured in a U.S. Food and Drug Administration (FDA)–registered establishment, using a quality system that complies with the FDA Quality System Regulation for Medical Devices and with the International Organization for Standardization (ISO) requirements designed for medical device companies. In addition, approximately 30 of Streck's products comply with European standards. Streck has gained 65 percent of the world market share for hematology controls through a combination of Streck label, private label, and patent licenses. Its products are marketed in 50 states and 42 countries. In Japan, Streck is the number one supplier of hematology reference controls.

Recognized as an innovator within its industry, the company owns more than 40 patents for clinical laboratory control products and continues to grow through acquisitions and partnerships.

Today, Streck designs controls for conducting immunophenotyping by flow cytometry. These products enable higher accuracy in monitoring patients, including those with the human immunodeficiency virus (HIV) that can lead to acquired immunodeficiency syndrome (AIDS). Streck also developed a transport reagent that preserves white blood cells and inactivates HIV so that patient samples are safe for technicians to handle. Streck strives to make a difference in the present and future of medical advances and health care.

Children's Hospital

This recognized leader in delivering health care for children brings together a friendly environment, pioneering physicians, high-tech equipment, and more than 25 specialty clinics, providing medical care ranging from the critical to the routine—and no one is turned away.

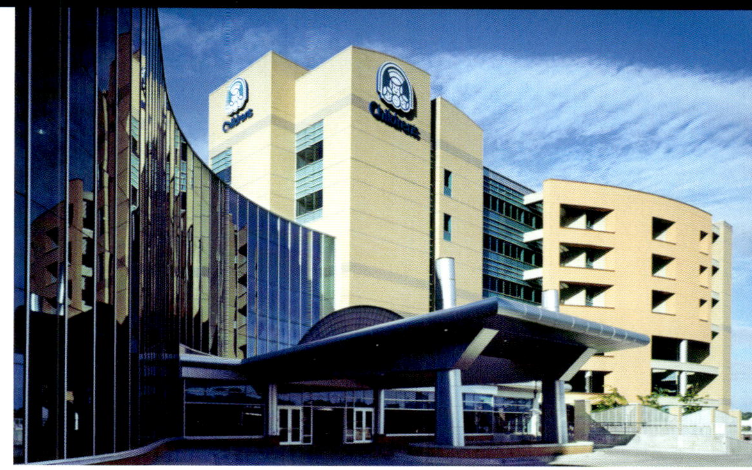

The vision of a Nebraska hospital dedicated to children was created in 1943 by the dean of the College of Medicine at the University of Nebraska, C. W. M. Poynter, M.D., and the publisher of the *Omaha World-Herald*, Henry Doorly. By 1948 the state's first and only children's hospital was built and opened for business.

Since then, Children's Hospital in Omaha has cared for children in the heartland. It has grown into a system of pediatric health care services that includes pediatric specialty clinics, a primary care pediatric group practice, home health services, and psychological counseling. It is the only pediatric hospital serving a region that includes Nebraska, southwest Iowa, and parts of Kansas, Missouri, and South Dakota. Under the direction of the dedicated community leaders on its board of directors, the hospital continues to grow, striving to ensure—according to its mission statement—"that all children may have a better chance to live."

Today, Children's Hospital is a 142-bed nonprofit health care facility with a staff of nearly 1,800. Some 7,200 pediatric inpatients were treated in 2005. Of these, 47 percent were from Omaha, 36 percent from elsewhere in Nebraska, and most of the remaining 17 percent from neighboring states. Patients are referred to the hospital for the treatment of complex or unusual diseases, as well as for pediatric primary care.

Children's Hospital is the primary inpatient teaching site for the joint Creighton University and University of Nebraska pediatric residency program. It also is the pediatric training site for the family practice residency programs at Clarkson Hospital, Creighton University and the University of Nebraska, and for many nursing and health professions schools and colleges.

More than 25 specialty clinics are operated by Children's Hospital, including hematology/oncology, diabetes, eating disorders, cardiology, allergy, developmental disabilities, and metabolic disorders. Round-the-clock in-house services are provided by pediatric critical care specialists and pediatric emergency medicine physicians. In 2005 the hospital served 5,200 outpatient surgery patients, and through its emergency department and two urgent care centers, it treated 38,000 children. New programs and services are continually added, such as its Eating Disorders program with inpatient, outpatient, and partial-day services; a Metabolic Management clinic; and the services of a nationally recognized bone specialist.

The hospital environment combines children's artwork and water and light features to produce a calm, healing atmosphere, and parents are encouraged to fully participate in their children's care. Additional information is provided by Children's Hospital on its Web site (www.chsomaha.org).

In 2005 and 2006 Children's Hospital was named one of the nation's Most Wired hospitals by *Hospitals & Health Networks* and in 2003, one of Omaha's best places to work by the Best Place To Work Institute and the Omaha Chamber of Commerce. The hospital also has been rated by *Child* magazine as one of the top children's hospitals in the nation.

Above left: Children's Hospital treats children who have complex or unusual diseases and also serves the community as a pediatric primary care facility. Above right: The design of the hospital's atrium incorporates water, light, and color, with artwork created by patients and area school children, to produce a calm, healing atmosphere.

PROFILES OF COMPANIES AND ORGANIZATIONS

Information Technology and Telecommunications

This outsourced communication solutions provider, headquartered in Omaha, Nebraska, creates customized customer contact solutions for its clients, allowing them to maximize the value of their customer interactions.

Above left: Renowned as a leading provider of outsourced communication solutions, West Corporation oversees its worldwide operations from its headquarters campus in Omaha. Above right: West uses call center agents as well as automated contact solutions to help its clients more effectively connect with their customers.

West Corporation is a leading provider of outsourced communication solutions to many of the world's largest companies, organizations, and government agencies. West operates more than 45 call centers and five automated voice and data centers in North America, Europe, and Asia. The company's integrated suite of customized solutions includes customer acquisition, customer care, automated voice services, public safety, conferencing, and accounts receivable management services.

Notably, West has been ranked among the top providers of outsourced communication solutions for all stages of customer interaction, including acquisition, retention, and growth. The company provides these services across many vertical markets, including financial services, health care, communications, insurance, and travel and hospitality, to name a few. By taking the time to understand each company it serves and the particulars of that company's industry, West is able to custom-tailor solutions that help its clients grow revenues, generate greater sales volumes, and maximize the profitability of existing customer relationships.

Communication Services

West's **Communication Services Group** supports its clients by offering call center agents, home-based contractors, business-to-business sales, outbound notifications, Internet, automated customer contact solutions, and public safety solutions. West represents its clients in customer care, customer service, sales, technical support, full account management applications, and emergency notification technology.

West Interactive provides automated customer contact solutions that allow callers to easily access information or conduct transactions via traditional or wireless telephones, hand-held devices, or the Internet. Callers may utilize either touch-tone or speech-response technologies, including natural language. West's automated call-processing platform is standards-based, open architecture that supports call control, computer-telephony integration (CTI), Voice over Internet Protocol (VoIP), and VoiceXML. West's clients benefit from seamless platform integration with their own corporate information systems, Web sites, and contact centers. These services ensure West Interactive clients superior operational flexibility and cost-reduction capabilities, as well as remote-access to obtain immediate call counts and customer survey results.

West Business Services provides customized business-to-business sales solutions that help companies maximize their sales and improve their market share. By combining its years of sales experience with innovative technology, West helps its clients streamline their operations, generate new sales, and manage qualified sales leads. West Business Services also helps its clients reduce costs by providing a full suite of business-to-business solutions that not only complement their existing sales force but also act as an extension of their business. West's proven systems and processes allow its clients to maximize productivity and reach more customers with greater frequency. West Business Services specializes in lead generation and management, direct sales, customer retention and growth, and customer win-back campaigns.

Intrado is North America's foremost provider of 9-1-1 emergency notification

systems and services and offers innovative solutions for telecommunications providers and public safety organizations. By acquiring industry leader Intrado in 2006, West gained the technology infrastructure and experienced management team needed to supply uninterrupted mission-critical emergency notification services to all major telecommunications providers in the United States.

West at Home is a remote-agent solution that provides a nationwide network of more than 11,000 high quality, well educated agents who process customer care and acquisition calls from their homes. West combines highly skilled agents with innovative technology to help companies across a wide range of industries improve scalability and flexibility while delivering superior care to their customers. The West at Home solution has been recognized with numerous awards and accolades, including the 2006 Frost & Sullivan Product Differentiation Innovation Award.

Conferencing Solutions

InterCall, a subsidiary of West Corporation, is the world's largest conferencing service provider. The company offers a wide range of services, from basic audio conferencing (conference calls) and online meetings to complex virtual events such as Webinars and video conferences. InterCall serves over 70,000 businesses worldwide with an extensive network of operations, sales, and support centers throughout North America, Europe, Australia, India, Latin America, and the Asia-Pacific regions.

Receivables Management

West's **Receivables Management Services** assists clients by custom-tailoring recovery programs for first-party and commercial collections, debt purchasing, government collections, and contingent/third-party collections. These services are provided to many of the nation's leading companies across a wide range of industries, including telecommunications, financial services, automotive, retail, manufacturing, utilities, health care, and transportation.

Technology Leadership

By investing in superior technology and cutting-edge systems, West has developed an industry leading, state-of-the-art customer contact infrastructure. West's customer contact systems are completely controlled and monitored through its Network Operations Center. This state-of-the-art facility allows for every call, transaction, and program to be monitored in real-time. Clients are able to access and utilize systems and stay ahead of the technology curve without making a significant capital investment.

Founded in 1986 and headquartered in Omaha, Nebraska, West has a team of 29,000 employees based in North America, Europe, and Asia. Recognized as one of the nation's top providers of communication services, West processes billions of minutes of telephone-related transactions annually for many of the nation's leading companies. The company's dedication to providing superior customer-contact solutions drives West to continually increase its processing capacity, develop innovative solutions, and maintain state-of-the-art technology to successfully meet its clients' growing needs.

Top left and top center: West's conferencing service provider InterCall offers a globally integrated suite of audio, Internet, and video conferencing options. InterCall serves more than 70,000 organizations worldwide. Top right, above, and above left: West's customer care support and full account management solutions are designed to help clients acquire, retain, and expand their customer relationships.

Nebraska Telecommunications Association

This statewide trade association represents Nebraska's private telecommunications companies before legislators and regulators to improve the availability and affordability of telecommunications for Nebraskans, rural and urban, and to advocate infrastructure growth to attract business to the state.

Above left: Nebraska telecommunications companies meet the needs of customers in every part of the state. Rural educational facilities particularly benefit from the services these companies provide. Above right: Nebraska telecommunications companies service a broad spectrum of customers, from individual residents to large corporations.

Nebraska's privately owned telecommunications companies have the cutting-edge capabilities to serve every business need, from those of Fortune 500 companies to those of home-based consultants. Nebraska enjoys a regulatory environment that has promoted investment in fiber-optic infrastructure and other telecommunications services throughout the state, and this environment has spawned the establishment and growth of companies that rely on an affordable, dependable, modern telecommunications network for success.

The Nebraska Telecommunications Association (NTA) promotes and represents the interests of Nebraska's telecommunications industry by presenting the views of its members to legislative and regulatory bodies. The NTA also informs and educates its stakeholders on current issues and programs and promotes a positive image of the industry.

Whether a business needs multiple lines for voice (Omaha is a national leader in telemarketing), high-volume broadband capabilities, or simply broadband availability (Nebraska has 100 percent coverage in high-speed Internet capability), Nebraska can meet any company's telecommunications demands.

A state with thickly populated urban areas and thinly populated rural ones, Nebraska poses diverse telecommunications challenges, and its telecommunications companies are as varied as its population. The one common feature these telecommunications providers share is high quality, state-of-the-art service no matter where in Nebraska their customers live.

More than 11,000 miles of fiber-optic cables are buried throughout Nebraska, serving the family rancher in the Sand Hills who sells beef internationally or the industry-leading insurance, architecture, engineering, agribusiness, and construction companies that employ thousands. No matter the need, Nebraska's network can meet it. That network is the backbone of a telecommunications system that carries data, voice, video, and any other application from Nebraska's businesses to the rest of the world and back.

Nebraska businesses are not the only customers for whom telecommunications are critical. The NTA's modern network brings medicine and education to even the most remote rural areas. The Nebraska Telehealth System allows doctors and health specialists to "visit" Nebraska communities every day. The network expands libraries' resources beyond their walls. Schools across the state connect through distance learning and share a single teacher located in a classroom miles away, using teachers and financial resources effectively. All these things are possible through the connections from Nebraska's telecommunications companies.

Whether a manufacturer needs large broadband data, a central office employing thousands needs large-capacity voice and broadband, or a consultant needs home-based Internet service, Nebraska's telecommunications companies welcome the chance to serve each with the same high quality that it provides its current customers.

PROFILES OF COMPANIES AND ORGANIZATIONS

Manufacturing

Kawasaki Motors Manufacturing Corp., U.S.A.

The first foreign vehicle manufacturing plant in the United States, this trendsetting operation, a subsidiary of a leader and innovator in personal recreation vehicles and lean-manufacturing processes, adds vigor to Nebraska's heavy-industry sector and economy as a whole.

Among midwestern states, Nebraska increasingly stands out for its manufacturing might. Much of its growth in manufacturing comes from the success of Kawasaki Motors Manufacturing Corp., U.S.A. (KMM).

The company is a subsidiary of Kawasaki Heavy Industries, Ltd., the renowned Kobe, Japan–based manufacturer founded in 1878. Kawasaki came to the Cornhusker State in 1974, planting roots in Lincoln, where it established a motorcycle plant and turned out its first unit nine months later.

In July 1975, the Lincoln plant launched production of the Jet Ski® watercraft, and between that and motorcycles, Kawasaki established a name for quality and innovation that continues to this day. The company's motorcycles are globally praised, and its watercraft products are an industry standard. The Jet Ski watercraft was a revolutionary invention that continues to delight millions of water-sports enthusiasts around the globe.

Kawasaki motorcycles and all-terrain vehicles (ATVs) carved out niches as fun, reliable recreational vehicles as well. Over the years, Kawasaki has also produced police bikes, as well as utility vehicles such as the popular four-wheel-drive Mule™, which is used in farming, construction, and other industrial jobs.

Quality in Motion

Since the mid 1970s, Kawasaki has expanded its product lineup to include light rail cars and industrial robots, and it has won praise for its production processes. Along the way, the manufacturer has developed a reputation as a quality leader in each industry in which it is a player.

The 1.7-million-square-foot Lincoln complex, sprawled over 335 acres, is the site of corporate offices, research and development facilities, manufacturing operations, and warehouse space. Today, along with manufacturing Jet Skis, ATVs, and Mules, the plant produces wheel rims for its own products and for some competitors. It also manufactures light rail cars; it makes parts for Kawasaki Construction Machinery Corp. of America, based in Kennesaw, Georgia; and it manufactures seats for subway cars that are assembled by Kawasaki Rail Car, Inc. of Yonkers, New York. Kawasaki's Lincoln facility has built robots that are used for welding, bonding, painting, ergonomics, and other industrial applications.

Kawasaki established a site in Maryville, Missouri, in 1989, where it produces small engines for consumer products, such as the ATVs that are assembled at the Lincoln site, and lawn mowers. The nearly 700,000-square-foot Maryville complex, less than 200 miles east of Lincoln, also has research and development facilities.

Right: The Kawasaki Motors Manufacturing Corp., U.S.A. complex in Lincoln includes manufacturing and warehouse space, research and development facilities, and administrative offices. The complex was opened in 1974.

Nearly 1,400 workers are employed at the Lincoln site, and the workforce in Maryville totals approximately 800. Every day, employees work hard to ensure that the products they make uphold the standard of quality for which Kawasaki has become known.

Employees are assisted by the unique Kawasaki Production System (KPS), a flexible workflow process that maximizes efficiency while minimizing wasted motion, and by the plant's just-in-time supply method, which allows cost-effective control of inventory.

KPS encourages employee input into quality assurance and the improvement of techniques that make processes and products better. Workers control conveyor operations and are provided with controls to instantly notify supervisors of potential problems in production and thus eliminate mistakes. Key points of the KPS are displayed prominently throughout the plant to remind the staff that "quality is everyone's responsibility." The system is so highly regarded that manufacturers across the country visit Kawasaki plants to learn more about KPS.

One of Lincoln's largest employers, Kawasaki has been recognized for contributing to the area's economy. The Nebraska Diplomats, Inc. gave Kawasaki its 2005 Industry of the Year award. The honor recognizes progressive Nebraska companies for their success, growth, and commitment to economic development in the state.

Kawasaki takes its role as a corporate citizen seriously and is a supporter of state colleges and universities. For instance, the company established the Kawasaki Reading Room for Japanese Studies at the University of Nebraska–Lincoln. The initiative promotes Japanese language and culture among students, the academic community, and Lincoln residents.

By producing high quality products, providing jobs, benefiting the economy, and doing its part to promote higher education, Kawasaki has become a welcome member of the Lincoln community. With the local economy steadily expanding, Kawasaki is on a smooth road on a clear day with the horizon beckoning.

Bottom left: Production of the Kawasaki Jet Ski® watercraft was launched in 1975 at the Lincoln manufacturing plant. Above left: The facility also manufactures recreational four-wheel-drive all-terrain vehicles (ATVs). Above right: The Lincoln complex includes a plant for light rail car manufacturing.

Behlen Mfg. Co.

Teamwork and value-added customer satisfaction continue to be the focus at this Columbus, Nebraska–based manufacturer, recognized for its ingenuity and vision, which for 70 years has been providing diverse products known around the world.

Above: Behlen Mfg. Co. "Partners In Progress" gather in front of the Columbus, Nebraska, world headquarters to celebrate the company's 70-year anniversary.

In 1936, Behlen Mfg. Co. was founded in the Columbus, Nebraska, garage of Walter D. Behlen. The company first made toe caps for work shoes and lid clamps for wooden egg crates. It soon gained a reputation for innovative, quality farm products such as grain tanks, corn cribs, and farm dryers. In 1950, the owners expanded their product line, offering grain bins and dryers and a self-framing building system.

In 1969, Behlen was sold to the Wickes Corporation, and in 1982 A. F. "Tony" Raimondo joined the company as general manager. After a major change in the grain industry in 1984, Raimondo led a management buyout and returned the company to local ownership.

Raimondo, now Behlen chairman and CEO, transformed the company culture from autocratic and hierarchical to participatory and honor-based. Today, Behlen is a company with strong people involvement, no time clocks, guidelines (versus rules), and a variable pay system of gain sharing and profit sharing. "The future looks bright at Behlen," says President and COO Phil Raimondo. "After surviving the manufacturing recession of 2000 to 2003, the focus on safety, quality, and productivity improvements has positioned the company to be capable of having the best year ever in 2006."

Today, over 1,000 "Partners In Progress" (Behlen employees) flourish in the Behlen culture of learning and involvement. At the heart of this culture is the company's system of mutual trust and respect—not only internally but with suppliers and customers as well. According to Phil Raimondo, "It is an exciting time to be part of this winning team."

The Diverse Business Units of Behlen

Behlen is organized into four business units, each with its own product line and marketing strategy. This diversity adds stability, flexibility, and growth opportunities.

- **Behlen Country** is the nation's largest manufacturer of livestock equipment. Products include farm gates, corral panels, livestock-handling equipment, horse stalls, dog kennels, livestock feeders, waterers, and water tanks. These products are sold to over 4,500 retail outlets throughout the United States, Canada, and Mexico. Behlen Country manufactures products in Columbus, Nebraska, and at Behlen plants in Huntington, Tennessee, and Baker City, Oregon.
- **The Building Group** consists of Behlen Building Systems, Inland Buildings, and Behlen China. Behlen Building Systems provides

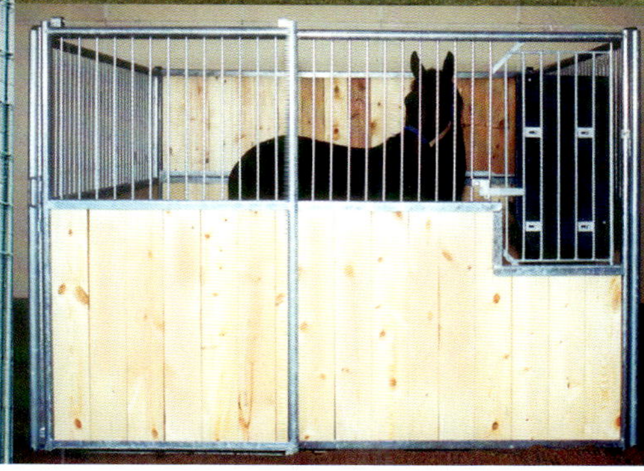

a wide variety of metal buildings for custom-designed projects. Inland Buildings serves the eastern half of the United States from its plant in Cullman, Alabama. Behlen China, a joint venture in northwest Beijing's Haiden District, provides Behlen Metal Building Systems to all segments of the growing China construction market.

- **International and Diversified Products** (IDP) consists of three product groups: International Agricultural Systems (one of the few remaining grain bin companies left in the country); Strip Joining Presses, used worldwide to join metal coils together in continuous line operations; and Custom Fabrication, which provides manufacturing services for local and regional customers.

- **BMC Transportation**, a Behlen subsidiary, is the company's dedicated truck fleet. Over 100 owner-operators work as ambassadors to Behlen customers across the country.

Behlen Mfg. Co. achieves exceptional customer service across the company's business units and provides outstanding quality through each unit's diverse product lines. The Behlen PRIDE Quality System stands for "Partners Responsible in Demonstrating Excellence." PRIDE represents the ISO 9001 certification that Behlen has maintained since 1999 at its Columbus, Nebraska, plant. This ISO 9001 certification confirms that Behlen meets or exceeds international quality standards. In 2000, Behlen won the prestigious Nebraska State Edgerton Quality Award of Excellence in Continuous Improvement, and in 2005 it won the Edgerton Quality Award of Progress.

The world headquarters of Behlen Mfg. Co., an 850,000-square-foot manufacturing facility in Columbus, Nebraska, exports products to over 70 countries. After signing a joint venture agreement in May 2002, Behlen Metal Buildings Engineering, Ltd. opened a plant in Beijing, China.

Behlen Mfg. Co. celebrates its 70th anniversary in 2006. By diversifying its product lines and adding value for customers, the company has adapted to a changing marketplace. The vision statement of Behlen, "Where Teamwork and Change Make Customers and Employees Better Off," is manifest when the company crosses traditional boundaries, like developing a participatory model of leadership.

The name Behlen stands for quality, continual improvement, and new ways to add value for customers.

Above, far left: These Behlen grain bins are in Clay Center, Nebraska. Top: Metal Building Systems, like the one used for this award-winning building, are made by Behlen and sold through a network of builders across the country. Above center, both photos Behlen Country, the leading U.S. manufacturer of livestock-handling equipment, sells horse stalls, livestock chutes, and other products throughout the United States, Canada, and Mexico. Above, far right: Behlen fabricated this top-quality dog kennel.

This global, multibillion-dollar industrial manufacturer has two plants in Nebraska—one in Kearney and one in Hastings—that make precision-machined automotive parts designed to deliver improvements in fuel economy, emissions, safety, and performance as well as fuel the passions of car drivers.

Above: Eaton Corporation's award-winning Eaton-Kearney plant supplies precision-forged and precision-machined valves and gears to original equipment manufacturers (OEMs) worldwide, including the corporation's Eaton-Hastings plant.

Eaton Corporation is a multinational manufacturer for markets spanning commercial and military aviation, aerospace, marine, trucks, passenger cars, agricultural equipment, industrial machinery, and residential, commercial, and industrial buildings. Founded in 1911 by J. O. Eaton with two partners, the company is headquartered in Cleveland, Ohio, and has operations around the globe. It sells its products to customers in 125 countries. With more than $11 billion in sales in 2005 and 59,000 employees worldwide, Eaton's revenues are created through four business segments—Electrical, Fluid Power, Truck, and Automotive.

Eaton Automotive, which has two plants in Nebraska, recorded nearly $2 billion in 2005 sales. Partnering with the passenger car and light truck industry, Eaton Automotive develops and manufactures innovations that fuel the passions of car buyers while delivering improvements in fuel economy, emissions, safety, and performance. Eaton Automotive manufactures engine valves, valve actuation systems, cylinder heads, differentials, mirror systems, fuel vapor controls, and various types of gears in facilities located throughout North and South America, Europe, and Asia.

Eaton-Kearney

Eaton Automotive began manufacturing engine valves at its plant in Kearney, Nebraska, in 1969, with 100 employees. The decision to build in Kearney was based in part on the strong work ethic, availability of space, and quality of life that colors the state. Since then, the plant has tripled in size and its staff has increased to 700, making the facility one of Eaton's most successful plants. Certified as an ISO 14001 and ISO/TS 16949 facility, Eaton-Kearney supplies precision-forged and -machined valves and gears to original equipment manufacturers (OEMs) worldwide, including Eaton-Hastings.

Today, the focus of Eaton-Kearney's engine valve business is passenger cars and light trucks. Since opening, the plant has remained true to the Eaton philosophy to be "accountable for its commitments and expect that its performance will be measured." Eaton-Kearney customers require on-time delivery, competitive pricing, and product performance—and Eaton delivers consistently.

Eaton-Kearney's gear business serves several market sectors, including agriculture, marine, heavy duty, all-terrain vehicles (ATVs), and automotive. Eaton-Kearney manufactures high quality gears backed by expert technical service, production flexibility, value pricing, and on-time delivery, the qualities that have come to distinguish Eaton among manufacturers.

Eaton's corporate philosophy embraces a culture in which employees can achieve their full potential to make exceptional contributions. The plant has an educated and experienced workforce, with all associates having at least a high school diploma or equivalent, and over 25 percent having higher education or degrees. Furthermore, Eaton-Kearney employees have an average of 14.5 years of experience at the plant.

Over the years, Eaton-Kearney frequently has been recognized for its efforts in safety and environmental performance. As a result of its efforts, the plant has achieved a rate 86 percent below the industry national average for

lost workday injury and illness, and has fewer recordable accidents than the average. In 1994, Eaton-Kearney was the company's first facility to receive the OSHA (Occupational Safety and Health Administration) Voluntary Protection Program (VPP) Star award. Today it is one of fewer than 150 businesses across the nation with nine or more years in the prestigious VPP program.

Eaton-Hastings

In 1997, Eaton Automotive determined that it needed another plant. It was drawn to Hastings, Nebraska, for the same reasons it came to Kearney. By 1998, the Hastings plant had 35 workers and was producing differential lockers. Today Eaton-Hastings, located just 35 miles southeast of Kearney, has more than 100 employees.

Eaton-Hastings builds differentials for automobiles, light trucks, and sport-utility vehicles (SUVs). It also machines gears and housing differentials and assembles them. Among its products is E-Locker, Eaton's innovative electronic locking differential made at Hastings. E-Locker allows drivers to lock their differential at the flip of a switch, channeling the engine's power to the wheels with traction.

Eaton-Hastings is ISO 14001 and ISO/TS-16949 certified, and in 2004, Eaton-Hastings received the Eaton Business Excellence (EBE) award, the highest level of achievement within the Eaton Corporation. The following year, Eaton-Hastings also received the EBE Division Excellence award, as well as the OSHA VPP Star award.

Eaton-Hastings considers its employees to be its greatest assets. It fosters a high-performance team environment with 11 cross-function teams that are actively involved in daily operations and strategic planning.

Eaton Values

Both Eaton Automotive Nebraska plants are active corporate citizens in the community. Notably, the Eaton Foundation, over the years, has contributed and continues to contribute financial support to numerous capital-building campaigns for the Museum of Nebraska Art, the Kearney Center for the Performing Arts, the Kearney Dinner Theater, the YMCA, the American Red Cross, and many other worthy organizations. The company also participates in Relay for Life, various food drives, and other community activities.

Employees also volunteer their time and talent as coaches for club sports; as Boy Scout and Girl Scout leaders; and as board members for the American Red Cross, United Way, and other humanitarian organizations in their areas.

In 2006, the Eaton-Hastings plant received the United Way Community Partnership Award for starting and participating in the 2-1-1 Program in Hastings. This program, with its easy-to-remember telephone number—211—connects callers to information about vital health and human services available in their community.

Embracing Eaton's core values and philosophy, both Eaton-Kearney and Eaton-Hastings continually strive for excellence—in their products, employee performance, customer satisfaction, work environment, and community involvement—as they look to the future.

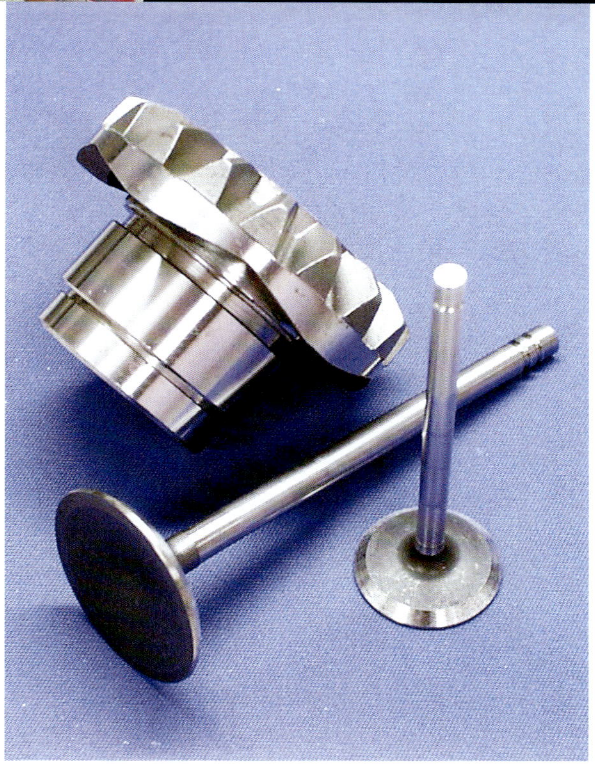

Top: Employees and their families enjoy Eaton's annual Health and Safety Fair.

Above: These are examples of Eaton's precision-forged gears and engine valves.

PROFILES OF COMPANIES AND ORGANIZATIONS

Professional and Business Services

This Omaha-based staffing and recruitment firm, one of Nebraska's leading employers, provides human capital management solutions to clients in all 50 states, placing thousands of talented professionals specializing in all kinds of business, from health care to finance.

Above: Shown here with C&A Industries, Inc. COO Scot Thompson (center) are division managers (from left) Cindy Shea of AurStaff, Chris Carlson of Aureus Group, Craig Wolf of Aureus Medical Group, and Patty North of Celebrity Staffing.

At C&A Industries, Inc., "people are the solution." Skilled, dedicated employees have not only made C&A Industries the company it is today; they are its core product—one that clients nationwide depend on in a competitive business environment.

Founded in 1969 by Larry Courtnage, C&A Industries began as a one-man operation securing engineers and architects for major firms throughout the Midwest. Courtnage, an engineering graduate of the University of Nebraska–Lincoln, sought to create a recruitment firm that operated in partnership with human resources departments and that focused on job specialization. In the following decades, C&A Industries became a leading provider of human capital management solutions for many industries, with clients in all 50 states.

This Omaha staffing and recruitment firm places supplemental, contract-hire, and direct-hire (full-time) workers in emerging, middle market, and Fortune 500 companies. It has offices in Lincoln, Nebraska; Kansas City, Missouri; and Des Moines, Iowa.

Growth and expansion into niche markets define the company today. C&A Industries comprises four staffing divisions that each bring specialized, in-depth market knowledge to employee searches, resulting in exceptional talent and less administrative strain for clients.

Three staffing divisions—the Aureus Group (which encompasses Aureus Finance & Accounting, Aureus Executive, and Aureus Systems), Celebrity Staffing, and AurStaff—are market leaders in Omaha and Lincoln, and C&A Industries also has a significant presence in Des Moines and Kansas City. The fourth staffing division, Aureus Medical Group, as well as Aureus Executive, the executive search arm of Aureus Group, serve clients nationwide.

The company's nonstaffing divisions are FocusOne Solutions, a managed services provider; AurTravel, a full-service travel agency; and AurHomes, which specializes in corporate housing.

A leading Nebraska employer, C&A Industries places thousands of workers throughout the United States. The U.S. Department of Labor's Bureau of Labor Statistics predicts that the staffing industry will be the country's fifth fastest-growing through 2012. C&A Industries will keep pace by expanding its internal workforce.

The company invests heavily in its internal staff. Each internal employee undergoes intensive training at Aureus University, an in-house state-of-the-art education and career development facility.

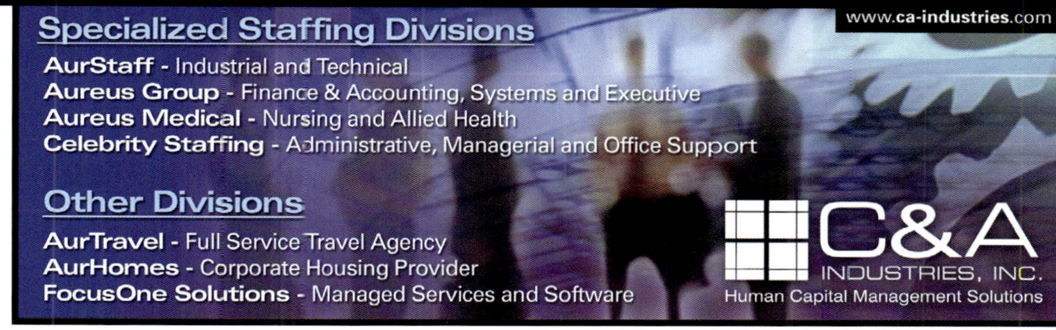

"We're a company that's committed to our people—giving them the tools they need to succeed and to develop their careers with us. The stronger and more skilled our employees are, the better they are able to deliver to our customers," says Courtnage.

A visionary, Courtnage firmly believes in the fundamental role that technology plays in business development. C&A Industries uses sophisticated systems and software to improve its processes and service delivery, and it even develops software of its own. One of Omaha's first businesses to computerize (in the early 1980s), C&A Industries has never strayed from the cutting edge and never plans to.

Technology leads to efficiency, which accelerates growth. For four consecutive years beginning in 2001, *Inc.* magazine listed C&A Industries as one of the country's 500 fastest-growing private companies. With annual revenues around $200 million and growing, C&A Industries is one of Omaha's largest employers and is the nation's 67th-largest staffing firm, according to the *Staffing Industry Report*, published by Staffing Industry Analysts, Inc. Aureus Medical Group is among the nation's top 10 health care staffing firms.

Giving back to the community is a core value at C&A Industries, and employees participate in philanthropy. The company supports health and human services organizations and has started its own, including the Kim Foundation, an advocacy group for the mentally ill, and Career OutReach, which helps people find jobs and acquire job skills.

C&A Industries knows what it takes to retain and develop its client base. Scot Thompson, chief operating officer, says, "When organizations turn to us, they're making an investment, and we take that responsibility seriously. As a company, we're dedicated to delivering the highest possible return and a premium level of service to each and every customer."

As a business leader and community partner, C&A Industries, Inc. would have it no other way.

Above left: Monica Fuehrer of Celebrity Staffing meets with Jonathan White to discuss career opportunities. Celebrity Staffing is a leading provider of administrative, office support, and managerial personnel in Omaha and Lincoln, Nebraska.

The Gallup Organization

Committed to researching human behavior and helping enterprises and individuals worldwide maximize productivity, this organization—well-known for its Gallup Poll—provides performance-management solutions and offers educational and degree programs at its universities, including its 50-acre riverfront campus in Omaha.

Above left: The Gallup Organization's Omaha Riverfront Campus serves as both the company's operational headquarters and a location for Gallup University consulting and seminars. Above right: Inside the atrium of Gallup's Omaha Riverfront Campus, visitors are welcomed by a mural of Gallup images throughout the years.

The Gallup Organization, one of the world's largest providers of research-based consulting, has studied human nature and behavior for more than 70 years. The company's 2,000 professionals, who excel in management, economics, psychology, and sociology, deliver the company's services at client locations, online via the Internet, and from 40 offices in 27 countries.

Gallup's consulting university builds from "The Gallup Path," a business model that links each employee's contribution to the organization's financial performance. It is a concept that resulted from more than 30 years of research into the factors that have the greatest impact on business performance.

"Gallup helps clients achieve maximum profitability by helping them better understand and engage their employees and customers," says Jane Miller, Gallup's chief operating officer.

Gallup University is one of the world's leading providers of management education to organizations and individuals, offering degree programs and continuing education. Its four main U.S. campuses are in Omaha; Chicago, Illinois; Irvine, California; and Washington, D.C., Gallup's world headquarters. Courses are also offered at many Gallup offices worldwide. Gallup provides organizations with the knowledge, strategies, and best practices needed to achieve improved performance.

Among Gallup University's offerings are the Great Manager Program, as well as courses on the demands of leadership and how to create a strengths-based organization. The 50-acre Gallup University Riverfront Campus in downtown Omaha is the center for Gallup University's executive and management training program. Gallup also works in partnership with the University of Nebraska–Lincoln to offer master of business administration and master of arts degrees with a specialization in executive leadership.

Since its inception, Gallup has shared its insights on public opinion polling, societal issues, and education. It now offers insights on management and human talent through publications and books by the Gallup Press. In 2002, the organization introduced a Web-based storage system to contain millions of records of what people have thought since 1935 and to provide ongoing opinion-tracking data. The system contains information such as consumer confidence, spending habits, household savings, fear of unemployment, and more.

Founder George Gallup, Ph.D., believed that the company's guiding principle should be independence of study and ultimately, objectivity. That simple principle, which has endured throughout the company's history, has given the Gallup Organization the credibility and trust of organizations around the world. For the future, Gallup is focused on continuing to educate, inform, and advise the world's most influential leaders.

Applied Information Management Institute

On the leading edge of workforce development, this nonprofit consortium of business, education, government, and community partners not only helps prepare students for careers, it also helps businesses compete in the global, information-based marketplace of the 21st century.

From the outset, the Applied Information Management (AIM) Institute had its sights set toward the future. Today it continues to maintain a forward-looking vision as it works closely with its members and across the community to identify the information technology (IT) needs of firms in the area. AIM then ensures that students have access to the curriculum and applied experiences necessary to develop the skills that businesses require to address these needs. Simply put, the mission of this nonprofit consortium is to provide IT leadership to Nebraska. AIM focuses, coordinates, and synergizes the resources of its partners to achieve these goals.

Nebraska, however, was not always so proactive. In the late 1980s, the Omaha business community suffered a crisis when a major oil company relocated its entire corporate headquarters from Omaha to Texas because of a labor shortage. The Greater Omaha Chamber of Commerce, along with business and community leaders, wisely recognized the need to better position Omaha and the entire state of Nebraska for future business and economic development. They commissioned several studies, and the resulting reports planted the seeds for AIM.

Since it was established in 1991, AIM has been relentless in its efforts to identify creative solutions to improve the development of an educated workforce, and to help Nebraska compete in the information-based global economy. AIM's services are focused on five strategic goals: to provide leadership in IT, to build a strong workforce, to improve the quality of IT education, to promote community growth, and to empower people through IT.

Robert E. Sweeney, Ph.D., AIM's founding director, reflects, "Since its beginning, AIM has been honored to work with business, education, government, and other leaders from across Nebraska and the region to develop and deliver an array of grant-based initiatives and quality fee-based services. The impact of these programs on literally thousands of people of all ages and backgrounds, and from all walks of life has been particularly rewarding."

The success of AIM is evident by its track record, numerous awards, and the proliferation of business within the state. Since inception, AIM has generated more than $23 million in grants that have supported the creation and continuation of its mission-related programs and services. Additionally, it has obtained nearly $43 million in grants for Omaha and Nebraska schools and community-based organizations. In 2005, Nebraska Governor Dave Heineman awarded AIM the Governor's Distinguished Leadership Award for Workforce Development.

As the economy becomes more deeply ingrained in global IT, the development of an educated workforce becomes more critical than ever. AIM plans to continue its efforts to address the labor shortage in the technology fields and to expand the pipeline of young talent to meet the demands of the workplace. Specific strategies include the ongoing enhancement of AIM's CareerLink online recruitment Web site as well as the establishment of a scholarship program for low-income, first-generation 8th-grade students—the AIM Achiever Scholarship Program.

Kandace R. Miller, president and chief executive officer of AIM, concludes, "Building on Dr. Sweeney's legacy, we look forward to providing continued service and relevance to support Nebraska and regional economic development around issues related to information technology."

Above: The Applied Information Management (AIM) Institute, a nonprofit consortium, provides information technology (IT) leadership to Nebraskans, preparing the state's future workforce for IT-related jobs and helping local businesses stay on the cutting edge of their industries.

Nebraska Department of Economic Development

This organization, Nebraska's leading economic development agency, capitalizes on the state's prime central location, excellent workforce, business-friendly climate, and quality of life to attract business and help homegrown businesses compete and succeed globally.

Above: Nebraska offers something for everyone. The challenging and scenic 18-hole Monument Shadows Golf Course—located at the base of Scotts Bluff National Monument in Gering—offers exceptional golf enhanced by outstanding views.

Truly a land of opportunities, the state of Nebraska boasts a central location, a quality workforce, a positive economic environment, and an exceptional quality of life. It may well be an unintentional secret ready to be revealed. If the initial response to the Nebraska Advantage Act—which took effect January 1, 2006—is any indication, the state's business climate clearly has positioned Nebraska to be a preferred location for starting and growing a business.

The Nebraska Advantage Act is incentive legislation that promotes growth through capital investment, innovation, and the creation of new jobs, as well as training for workers who take those jobs.

Spearheading this growth is the state's lead economic development agency, the Nebraska Department of Economic Development (NDED). Created by the Nebraska Legislature in 1967, NDED has a clear and simple objective: to grow and diversify the state's economic base. Its mission is to promote and foster economic opportunities that will enable businesses and communities to compete, grow, and succeed.

Richard Baier, NDED director, reflects, "Nebraska is known for its great work ethic and business-friendly atmosphere. It is a great place to live, work, play, and grow a business. The possibilities in our state truly are endless, and we are right in the 'center of it all.' The department's many programs and services really support communities' development efforts; help start, retain, and expand businesses; promote the state for business locations and expansions; and encourage increased visitations by travelers."

To achieve these ambitious goals, the NDED is divided into four operating divisions to better address each target area.

- The Business Development Division assists communities with business and economic development programs, and it represents statewide interest in recruiting businesses to Nebraska. Its portfolio of programs includes One-Stop Business Assistance, International Trade and Investment, Job Training, and the Business Visitation Program.
- The Community and Rural Development Division provides technical and financial services through community-targeted programs. These include grant programs for the Nebraska Microenterprise Development Program, the Community Development Assistance Act tax incentive program, and for housing, community infrastructure, planning and business development.
- The Travel and Tourism Division promotes this steadily expanding industry within the state. Revenue from Nebraska's one percent lodging tax has increased every year since 1981. In 2005, travelers spent almost $3.1 billion in Nebraska, and the industry has created some 43,000 Nebraska jobs.
- The Administration and Operations Division supports the other three operating divisions with cost-effective administrative, fiscal, human resources, marketing, and public information services.

Through the concerted efforts of the NDED, an increasing number of companies in the United States and around the world are discovering that Nebraska offers a wealth of resources and opportunities for businesses to grow and succeed.

Capitol building, Lincoln

PROFILES OF COMPANIES AND ORGANIZATIONS

Real Estate, Development, and Construction Services

As one of the leading owners and managers of commercial properties in the United States, this unique full-service, strategic commercial development company has built a portfolio of more than 100 projects that span 17 states across the country.

Above: Noddle Companies provides a full range of property development and management services, from site acquisition through financing, construction, and property management. Among the company's many landmark Omaha projects is the Midwest regional headquarters of the National Parks Service (above). Right: Omaha's Harvey Oaks shopping center is among the more than 85 shopping centers developed or purchased by Noddle Companies in 16 states.

Stability, integrity, dependability—all three are synonymous with Noddle Companies. And all three are consistent with the company's approach since Harlan J. Noddle started the company in 1971 in Omaha, Nebraska. From the very beginning, Noddle and his partner, Joseph Kirshenbaum, sought high quality development projects that were not only profitable but also beneficial to the community as a whole.

Since its first project was completed in 1973 in Omaha, Noddle Companies has built or acquired an expansive portfolio of more than 100 projects nationwide. Perhaps more significant than the vast number, each project is now a functional and integral part of its surrounding community.

Unique Perspective

The consistent success of Noddle Companies may best be attributed to its unique approach to both clients and properties. From the outset, Noddle Companies has viewed its customers not as clients but rather as partners.

President and CEO Jay B. Noddle, son of the founder, says, "Noddle Companies was built on the belief that the best business relationships are based on mutual trust and profitability. Just as our properties are built on a solid foundation, we like to believe that our client relationships are, as well."

Beyond its relationships with clients, Noddle Companies also takes a unique approach to each property, regarding it as an individual investment capable of providing increasing returns. Noddle Companies consistently maximizes returns through creative solutions and strategic, proactive management tactics.

Comprehensive Services

This unwavering commitment to its clients and innovative solutions are bolstered by the company's comprehensive array of commercial real estate services. As clients' needs dictate, Noddle Companies can provide sophisticated development, consulting, and implementation services. From site selection, acquisition, master planning, and architect and contractor selection to contract negotiation, zoning, infrastructure installation, risk management, and construction management, Noddle Companies

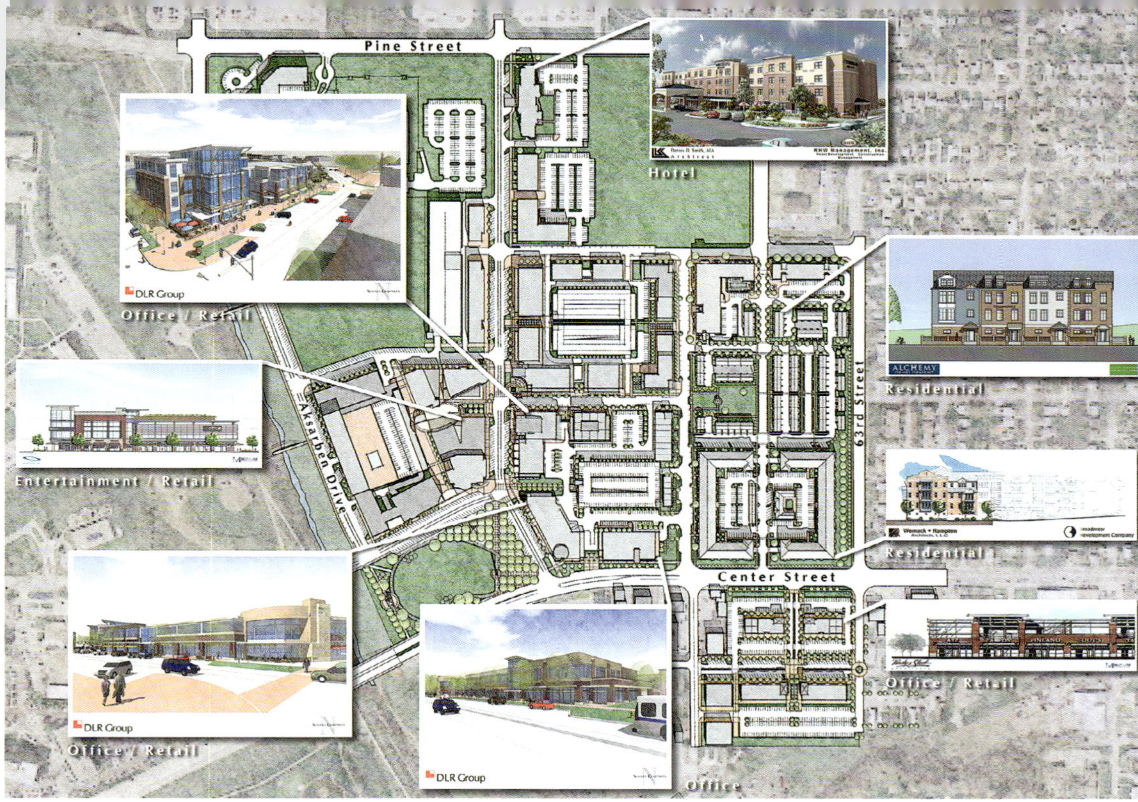

is able to pull a project together with expertise and innovation.

Track Record of Successes

With a special emphasis on urban and suburban retail and corporate centers, Noddle Companies and its senior staff have a solid track record of projects that range from 50,000 to one million square feet. Its portfolio includes some of Omaha's most notable landmarks, including One Pacific Place, the Gallup University Riverfront Campus, Security National Bank headquarters at Three Pacific Place, the Midwest regional headquarters of the National Park Service, and Aksarben Village, now under development.

Founder Harlan Noddle always felt a strong responsibility to the welfare of the community, particularly Omaha. Today, Noddle Companies carries on that responsibility with a management team that is actively involved in local, state, and national business and civic organizations, as well as the Omaha By Design Initiative, University of Nebraska–Omaha Business Strategic Planning Council, and numerous other organizations throughout Nebraska.

Noddle Companies built its reputation—and success—on stability, integrity, dependability, and commitment to the community. If history is any indication, the company will continue to follow this path in the years to come.

Above left: This rendering depicts Aksarben Village in Omaha, a 70-acre urban, mixed-use community being developed by Noddle Companies that includes office, retail, entertainment, and residential spaces. Construction began in 2006 and is being completed in phases over seven to 10 years. Above right: Noddle Companies also developed the Empire Fire & Marine Insurance Company building in Omaha.

This award-winning, full-service architectural, engineering, planning, and design firm specializes in built environments for corporate, educational, justice, sports, and entertainment clients, focusing on the unique goals of each client and the needs of those who will use the completed facility.

Above: The Ron & Carol Cope Stadium of the University of Nebraska at Kearney is one example of the award-winning projects completed by DLR Group.

DLR Group is a dynamic, client-focused design firm that demonstrates innovation and creativity in every aspect of its business. From its history as one of the first employee-owned organizations in its field to its reputation for projects that showcase its entrepreneurial spirit, the company is noted for its originality and design excellence. In 2005 alone, DLR Group received two dozen design awards from professional, client, and trade associations, affirming the exceptional ability of its project teams to create, plan, and execute extraordinary designs and inspiring solutions.

While DLR Group has an operating philosophy of decentralization, with the close-to-the-client style of a small firm and no official headquarters site, its roots are in Omaha. In 1962 Irving R. Dana, FAIA, began a full-service architectural and engineering firm that soon expanded to include associated services, such as technology planning and design and public-private partnerships. DLR Group's steadfast commitment to strong design, excellent service, client satisfaction, and employee ownership made growth and success inevitable.

In 1974 DLR Group acquired the Phoenix, Arizona, firm of Lescher and Mahoney, specialists in Southwestern architecture, to serve clients in the region. In 1986 the acquisition of another firm well-known in its area—John Graham Associates of Seattle, Washington—brought further geographic diversity, enabling DLR Group to continue expanding its reach while benefiting from the experience and stability of these noted design firms.

Over the years, DLR Group's impressive growth has been facilitated by the recruitment, development, and retention of talented people who are team-oriented, who possess excellent people skills, and who have a strong work ethic. Dale Hallock, one of DLR Group's managing principals, notes, "Our clients are our most important focus, and our people are our most valuable resource. It is the endorsement of our clients that has positioned us as leaders in our practice areas." *World Architecture* magazine agrees, ranking DLR Group as the world's largest criminal justice architecture practice nearly every year from 1999 to 2006.

In Omaha, DLR Group's creative design expertise and willingness to take a new approach can be seen in the Qwest Center Omaha convention center and arena. A significant addition to the redevelopment of the downtown area, the center was designed to create an exciting urban form, celebrating people, events, and the city and gracing the skyline in a single soaring gesture. The building is a fine example of DLR Group's high regard for the function of each project, and the facility has received national recognition.

In addition to its offices in Omaha, Phoenix, and Seattle, DLR Group has locations in Portland, Oregon; Sacramento, California; Colorado Springs, Colorado; Chicago, Illinois; Des Moines, Iowa; Overland Park, Kansas; Minneapolis, Minnesota; Philadelphia, Pennsylvania; Orlando, Florida; and Honolulu, Hawaii—with approximately 500 employee-owners nationwide.

Qwest Center

This innovative firm, with Nebraska offices in Omaha and Lincoln, provides custom-tailored solutions for commercial real estate owners, corporate occupants, and investors across the nation and around the world.

Above: A "Class A" office building, Grubb & Ellis|Pacific Realty's 127,848-square-foot One Pacific Place in Omaha is about a 15-minute drive from downtown.

Grubb & Ellis|Pacific Realty takes a keen interest in not only understanding the commercial real estate market but also knowing its dynamics and nuances. Grubb & Ellis|Pacific Realty takes this knowledge and custom-tailors it for clients, including sellers, buyers, lessors, and tenants, in order to provide them with comprehensive services.

These services begin with assessing the client's needs, analyzing the market, and developing a strategic real estate solution. Grubb & Ellis|Pacific Realty prides itself on taking the time to get to know its clients and carefully studying all the factors related to the client's situation before establishing a real estate plan. Its focus on providing all-inclusive services is something the company has emphasized from the start.

Early Expansion

The company was started in 1987 when Jay Noddle founded Pacific Realty Group in Omaha, with the goal of providing comprehensive commercial real estate services in the Midwest. Noddle hired a capable and committed team of real estate professionals to support his endeavors, and the enterprise soon grew into a sophisticated advisery, development, and consultation company providing a range of services for a variety of clients. In 1997, to enhance and expand the services it offered, Pacific Realty joined forces with Grubb & Ellis, one of the nation's largest commercial real estate and property management firms, forming Grubb & Ellis|Pacific Realty.

Integrated Services

Today Grubb & Ellis|Pacific Realty has a staff of 100 employees and serves a variety of property types, with sizes ranging from 2,500 to one million square feet. The company also manages property (a total of seven million square feet) and leases property (over four million square feet). Grubb & Ellis|Pacific Realty provides transaction advisory and management services, while Pacific Realty Group provides development and consulting services. Another arm of the company, Pacific Realty Mortgage, provides financing.

In addition to its Omaha base, Grubb & Ellis|Pacific Realty has a full-service office in Lincoln, Nebraska, and there are numerous Grubb & Ellis affiliate organizations across the United States.

The gamut of commercial real estate services provided by the company includes brokerage; lease administration and tenant representation; office, industrial, and retail leasing and sales; asset management; comprehensive development services; real estate tax consulting; tenant finished construction supervision; and construction and permanent-financing services.

In addition, Grubb & Ellis|Pacific Realty offers its clients a strong base

of business and professional affiliations that are a source of the most up-to-date information and services in the local, regional, national, and international marketplace. Some of the company's professional affiliations are the Building Owners and Managers Association (BOMA), Building Owners and Managers International (BOMI), the International Council of Shopping Centers (ICSC), the Society of Industrial and Office Realtors (SIOR), and the National Association of Corporate Real Estate Executives (NACORE).

Grubb & Ellis|Pacific Realty's commitment to service is exemplified in the outstanding performance of its employees. Each year, the company presents Circle of Excellence awards to its top 100 producers nationally—individuals who have achieved success by putting clients' needs first, being team players, and being experts in their local markets. Candidates for the designation must meet strict benchmarks and also demonstrate a commitment to philanthropic and community organizations. Honorees in Nebraska for 2005 included Allan Murow, Frank Barber, and Scott Heider.

Reaching Out

Committed to philanthropic endeavors, in 1990 Grubb & Ellis|Pacific Realty founded Pacific Pals to put opportunities for "kid stuff" into the lives of children who may not otherwise have them. Volunteers assist Pacific Pals in making a difference in the children's lives. Since it began, the program has helped more than 50,000 children and their families enjoy such activities as summer camps and university sporting events and places such as the Henry Doorly Zoo, the Omaha Ballet, Fontenelle Forest Nature Center, Omaha Children's Museum, the Joslyn Art Museum, and the Rose Blumkin Performing Arts Center.

With a true passion for the commercial real estate industry and a commitment to service, Grubb & Ellis|Pacific Realty continues to meet and exceed its clients' expectations with its skill, knowledge, and professionalism.

Grubb & Ellis|Pacific Realty represents some of Omaha's prime commercial real estate. Above left: Crossroads Crossing is located at one of Omaha's hottest intersections, 72nd and Dodge streets. Above right: Omaha's Rockbrook Village, where West Center Road meets Interstate 680, comprises upscale boutiques and restaurants.

PROFILES OF COMPANIES AND ORGANIZATIONS

Retail and Sales

Purveyor of the highest quality beef that comes straight from America's heartland, this manufacturer and distributor of premium steaks—plus pork, poultry, and seafood, and gourmet dishes from appetizers to desserts—lives up to its reputation for fine quality products and its commitment to customer satisfaction.

Above left: Omaha Steaks, Inc. has been headquartered in Omaha, Nebraska, since 1917. Above center: The Simons started their business in a building at 17th and Douglas streets in Omaha and sold their tender, grain-fed Midwestern beef to local restaurants and grocers. Above right: The company's famous steaks and other flavorful gourmet foods are carefully packed in dry ice and shipped in weatherproof, reusable insulated coolers.

Family owned since it was founded in 1917, Omaha Steaks, Inc. is a cut above the competition. Its products are shipped to customers around the world, and its highly efficient facilities are visited by meatpackers from as far away as Russia.

The Production of Quality

Omaha Steaks is famous for its grain-fed Midwestern beef, which is naturally aged, hand-trimmed, individually vacuum-wrapped, and flash-frozen. The company also offers veal, pork, lamb, and poultry; classic pastas; sauces and seasonings; side dishes, appetizers, and desserts; and even pet treats, plus cookbooks and gift ideas.

The company is known for its fast and friendly expert service. A constant stream of orders is received by telephone, by mail, and, since 1995, via the Internet through its Web site (www.omahasteaks.com), from individual customers as well as business incentive and foodservice buyers. The company also has some 80 of its own retail Omaha Steak Shops located across the country.

Omaha Steaks is headquartered in Omaha and operates three manufacturing plants, a freezer warehouse, and two distribution centers in the greater Omaha area. More than 1,800 dedicated employees share in Omaha Steaks' success and work diligently to guarantee customer satisfaction. The production management staff and product development team work together to develop the highest quality and variety, while making customer convenience a priority. Plant sanitation and food safety are of paramount importance in the company's manufacturing processes, and all products exceed U.S. Department of Agriculture standards.

Omaha Steaks rewards its employees for their devotion to quality by providing benefits packages and family-friendly policies that have won national recognition. The company has also received many awards and honors, including MassMutual's National Family Business of the Year award; Better Business Bureau's business integrity award; induction into the Greater Omaha Chamber of Commerce Business Hall of Fame; and recognition from the Nebraska Food Industry Association (NFIA) for the Simon family's lifetime of outstanding leadership.

Then and Now

The Omaha Steaks story began with Latvian immigrant J. J. Simon, who came to the United States with his wife and son to start a new life. Traveling west by train, when the family reached Omaha it reminded them of the farm country they had come from, and they decided to make it their new home. After working in several local markets, Simon and his son began their own company in cattle processing—the only business they knew. Named the Table Meat Supply Company, it gained a reputation for superior cuts of beef loin, ribs, boneless strips, and rib eyes. The business grew and moved to larger quarters, a trend that would repeat itself as more and more restaurants and grocers requested its flavorful grain-fed beef.

Today, Omaha Steaks supplies more than 2 million active buyers worldwide. Its outstanding products and service support Nebraska's reputation for high quality beef that comes straight from America's heartland. Now owned and operated by the fourth and fifth generations of the Simon family, Omaha Steaks is a success story that keeps growing, as Omaha Steaks continues its founders' tradition of excellence.

Oriental Trading Company, Inc.

With more than 25,000 value-priced toys, novelties, and party supplies, this dynamic direct marketer takes pride in creating fun—whether for a business or private occasion, school function, or any other event—by selling products through its popular catalogs and Internet retail sites.

Oriental Trading Company, Inc. (OTC) is in the business of fun. This direct marketer of value-priced toys, novelties, party supplies, crafts, and home décor has become an industry leader and one of the nation's top catalog and Internet retailers. From pink flamingos, yo-yos, and grass skirts to holiday decorations, scrapbooking supplies, and do-it-yourself crafts, OTC has something fun for everyone.

"We've come a long way from the days when we were primarily a toy and novelty cataloger," says CEO Steve Frary. "But our mission remains the same—to delight our customers with an irresistible assortment of fun products for every occasion. Our customers are the real heroes—they bring smiles to others by using our products to celebrate special occasions, events, and holidays."

Growing Fun

Based in Omaha since it began in 1932, OTC was one of the nation's first wholesalers of value-priced novelties and gifts. The company became a major supplier to the U.S. carnival trade in the 1950s before expanding in the 1970s by using catalogs and direct marketing to target consumers, retailers, and businesses. In the 1980s, OTC introduced a toll-free telephone number and launched seasonal catalogs nationwide. As use of the Internet grew in popularity in the late 1990s, OTC found a new vehicle to reach its ever-growing number of customers.

Today OTC is a leader in both Internet and catalog sales. *Catalog Age* rates OTC among the top 50 U.S. direct marketers, and *Internet Retailer* ranks it among the top 50 U.S. Internet retail sites. Through more than 40 catalog editions and three Web sites, OTC sells over 25,000 products to meet the needs of businesses, nonprofit groups, individuals, schools, churches, and teachers.

Keys to Success

OTC owes much of its success to its long-standing Asian sourcing relationships, its in-house design capability, its exceptional customer service, and the hard work of its employees. Additionally, outstanding civic cooperation and pro-business policies in state and local governments have made Nebraska a great place for the company to do business.

"Our location provides access to major highways and railroad hubs, making it easy for us to serve our customers," Frary says. "The state also offers a high quality, dedicated workforce." In return, OTC has brought the state more than 2,500 jobs.

A Bright Future

OTC's growth shows no signs of stopping. That growth will be supported by the expansion and automation of its La Vista warehouse, which at over 700,000 square feet is one of Nebraska's largest buildings.

"In 2007, Oriental Trading Company celebrates its 75th anniversary. Our goal is to make the world more fun," Frary says, "and that will always be at the heart of our mission."

For additional information or to order products, visit the company's Web site at www.orientaltrading.com.

Above, both photos: Oriental Trading Company, Inc. offers more than 25,000 products that bring smiles to every occasion throughout the year.

By combining the convenience of Internet technology with old-fashioned customer service, impeccable quality, and attractive prices, this longtime mainstay of Omaha has expanded its loyal customer base across the globe.

When renowned investor Warren Buffett made Borsheims part of Berkshire Hathaway Inc. in 1989, he said, "If you don't know jewelry, know your jeweler." Buffett—and people throughout the world—know Borsheims. With a history that spans more than a century, a facility that covers more than 62,000 square feet, an inventory that includes more than 100,000 pieces, and an international clientele across 50 states and five continents, Borsheims is one of the world's most renowned jewelers.

It began in 1870 when Louis Borsheim opened a small jewelry store in downtown Omaha. The arrival of the new transcontinental railroad a few years earlier and Nebraska's statehood status was turning the once rough-and-tumble town into a city—bringing with it a new interest in culture and demand for fine goods within the region.

From its location in the heart of downtown Omaha, Borsheims served the demands of an expanding community. In 1948, Louis Friedman and his son Ike purchased the business and maintained the name Borsheims—ushering in a new era of success for the jewelry store.

Ike Friedman, a dynamic businessman, developed a business philosophy for Borsheims that still guides the company today: "Offer an extensive inventory selection and a friendly style of customer service, at the lowest possible price.

By 1986, Borsheims had outgrown its 8,000-square-foot facility downtown and moved to the anchor position in Regency Court. In 1989, when Warren Buffett's Berkshire Hathaway purchased a majority of the company, Ike's dream of turning the company into a major, world-renowned jewelry retailer had become reality within his lifetime.

Because Susan M. Jacques worked closely with Ike for many years, it was only fitting that she should take the reins of this remarkable jewelry store. Since 1994, she has managed the business, following the same philosophy Ike developed.

From the late 1800s through the 21st century, the legendary success of Borsheims has known no bounds. As the store expands its facilities once again, it also extends its reach through the use of modern-day Internet technology that enables it to continue to foster a unique and unwavering loyalty from its customers worldwide.

That speaks largely to a philosophy that is keenly focused on providing customers with selection, service, and "The Borsheims Price"—just as it has been since its founding in 1870.

Right: Borsheims Fine Jewelry, an Omaha institution with a worldwide clientele, invites people to experience the world of luxury and timeless treasures. In 2006 Borsheims remodeled its only store location, in the Regency area of Omaha. With more than 62,000 square feet of shopping space, it is one of the largest jewelry stores in the nation.

PROFILES OF COMPANIES AND ORGANIZATIONS

Tourism and Hospitality

Close to numerous major corporate headquarters and world-class shopping, restaurants, and nightlife, this comfortable and luxurious hotel serves business and leisure travelers with a full range of amenities and also offers meeting rooms and large ballrooms for singular events.

Above left: The Crowne Plaza Hotel–Omaha offers its guests numerous amenities and services, such as its Sleep Advantage program, which features extremely comfortable beds, guaranteed wake-up calls, quiet-zone floors, and special amenities for a good night's sleep. Above center: Well-appointed guest rooms feature items for enhanced comfort, including bathrobes, as well as beds with upgraded mattresses, multiple pillows, and luxurious duvets and sheets. Above right: Guests are greeted by a friendly staff in the hotel's lobby, which offers informal meeting areas and comfortable seating.

"The Place to Meet" in Omaha is the Crowne Plaza Hotel–Omaha. From its exceptional location in burgeoning west Omaha to its 223 impressive guest rooms, including 11 guest suites, this well-appointed property is one of Nebraska's finest. Yet what makes the hotel stand out is the unsurpassed personal attention that guests receive from the moment they walk through the door.

The only Crowne Plaza in the state, the hotel offers all travelers outstanding services, such as its unique Sleep Advantage program. This initiative is designed to help guests have an optimal night's sleep and includes deluxe features such as duvets, luxurious sheets, sleep-inducing compact disks (CDs), and other sleep amenities. While the hotel was extensively renovated in 1999, its continual upgrades are what has brought the property back to the landmark status it enjoyed in the late 1970s.

From ceiling to floor, guest room to meeting room, swimming pool area to restaurant, all facets of the hotel were updated during its renovation. Complimentary high-speed Internet access is available in every guest room and meeting room, and there is a full-service, 24-hour business center, a health and fitness facility on-site, and an oversize swimming pool and whirlpool spa area that offers one of the best views of Omaha.

Furthermore, residents throughout the city, as well as visitors to Omaha, can take advantage of the Crowne Plaza's 10,000 square feet of flexible meeting space, divided among nine different rooms. Whether a group needs a comfortable boardroom for 12 or a large ballroom that can accommodate more than 300 people, the hotel can handle this and every size in between. It also offers one of the most experienced banquet staffs and has some of the area's best chefs.

Without a doubt, the Crowne Plaza's entire staff of more than 100 people, many of whom are multilingual, is dedicated to making every guest's stay not only comfortable but also enjoyable. As soon as guests arrive, they can easily see that staff members enjoy their work—this comes through in everything they do. Whether they are helping a local company hold a successful conference or cheering on the next College World Series team, the Crowne Plaza Hotel–Omaha's staff loves being part of their guests' successes.

This world-class exhibition hall and arena complex hosts major collegiate sporting events, books A-list performers, and offers plentiful meeting and convention space for business affairs, helping Omaha become a top destination for visitors from around the state and across the country.

Above: The contemporary Qwest Center Omaha adds new vitality and sophistication to the city's downtown riverfront district. This massive complex, which hosts NCAA, Big 12, and Olympic events, has consistently ranked as a Top 20 ticket-selling arena worldwide.

Qwest Center Omaha holds the record for the largest public works project in Nebraska. The venue development site occupies 422 acres, the equivalent of approximately 100 city blocks, and serves as the centerpiece of downtown Omaha's $2 billion riverfront revitalization project. The extraordinary arena and convention center—which open their doors to millions of guests each year—are major contributors to the economies of the City of Omaha and the State of Nebraska.

Qwest Center Omaha construction began in spring 2001 after Omaha voters approved bonds to fund the project. Completed in 2003, the center cost a total of $291 million, funded through a combination of public bonds, private donations, and $14 million from Qwest Communications. Since its opening, Qwest Center Omaha has changed the face of the city and the community. In fact, more than a million people visited the center during its first nine months of operations. The venue hosted the 2005 NCAA Division I women's volleyball regionals and was selected to host the 2008 NCAA men's basketball first- and second-round tournaments, the NCAA 2006 and 2008 Division I women's volleyball championship, the NCAA 2010 Division I wrestling championship, as well as the 2008 U.S. Olympic Team swim trials.

Qwest Center's exhibition hall covers 194,000 square feet, and its arena contains approximately 18,300 seats. A skywalk attaches the venue to Nebraska's only AAA four-diamond hotel, the 450-room Hilton Omaha. Qwest Center also provides about 4,500 parking spaces.

This huge investment in Omaha's future is paying dividends. Since the arena's opening, *Pollstar* magazine has consistently ranked Qwest Center Omaha as a Top 20 ticket-selling arena in the world. Qwest Center Omaha has outsold arenas such as the Staples Center in Los Angeles, California; the Pepsi Center in Denver, Colorado; plus arenas in London, England; Vancouver, British Columbia; and Munich, Germany. Qwest Center Omaha was nominated as a Best New Major Concert Venue in 2005 and was chosen as the Best Convention Center in 2006 by *Meetings MidAmerica,* a trade publication.

Qwest Center Omaha has proven to be a cornerstone for the economy and the people of Omaha, Nebraska. "Being part of the effort to put Omaha on the map as a world-class destination for millions of visitors has been thrilling," says Roger Dixon, president and CEO of Qwest Center Omaha. "We are proud to provide this venue for all of our guests, and we thank the community for their support."

Nebraska Mavericks at Qwest Center Omaha

PROFILES OF COMPANIES AND ORGANIZATIONS

Transportation and Distribution

Raw entrepreneurialism drove Clarence Werner to start his trucking business half a century ago; hard work, technology, and talented employees did the rest, turning a one-man, one-truck enterprise into a cutting-edge truckload carrier—one of the nation's five largest—whose fleet moves goods from coast to coast.

Above: Werner Enterprises, Inc.'s fleet of trucks moves freight such as retail merchandise, consumer products, food and paper products, beverages, industrial products, and building materials throughout the United States. This company also conducts business in Canada, Mexico, and China.

At age 19, Clarence L. Werner bought a Ford truck, using his car as a down payment, and started his own trucking business, hauling exempt commodities for larger trucking companies. Today, Werner Enterprises, Inc. is an interstate and intrastate general commodities carrier and logistics company. One of the five largest truckload carriers in the country, Werner also conducts business in Canada, Mexico, and China.

From its headquarters in Omaha, Werner's skilled and experienced management team leads more than 14,000 employees and independent contractors. The Werner fleet—almost 9,000 tractors and nearly 25,000 trailers—moves freight such as retail merchandise, consumer products, food and paper products, beverages, industrial products, and building materials.

Innovation and technology have helped unlock success for the company. Founder Werner directed the in-house team of computer specialists to develop technology to improve safety and eliminate the cumbersome paper logbooks that drivers used to plan and record their work hours and activities. The result was Werner's Paperless Log System, which was built as a feature of the company's satellite tracking system. The Paperless Log System is designed to ensure that drivers comply with federal regulations, undergo fewer complications and potential delays, and consequently stay with the company longer.

Werner has one of the best safety ratings among the 15 largest U.S. trucking companies. As a rule, its drivers are on time and avoid accidents. In 2003, the American Trucking Association named a Werner driver, Herb McArthur, as a captain of its America's Road Team—the third Werner driver to receive this honor.

"Werner strongly supports its drivers in educating the public on highway safety. I am honored to be one of the many 'Ambassadors of Safety' for Werner," says McArthur, a million-mile, accident-free driver.

Chairman and CEO Werner began his enterprise in 1956; today, two of his sons work for the company. Greg Werner is president and chief operating officer of the company, and Gary Werner is vice chairman. In June 1986, with a fleet of 630 trucks, Werner Enterprises, Inc. became a publicly traded company (NASDAQ: WERN).

The company has won industry awards for performance, community involvement, and safety, including the 2006 ShopKo Supply Chain All-Star award; the 2005 Target Mission Impossible Award; the 2005 Home Depot Partnering for Excellence Award; the 2005 Colgate-Palmolive Above and Beyond Carrier of the Year award; and the 2005 Wal-Mart Strive for Excellence Award in Customer Service. *Industrial Distribution* magazine has presented Werner with its annual Quest for Quality Carrier Award seven times in the past nine years. And in a 2003 *Industrial Distribution* survey representing thousands of shippers, Werner was the highest rated among U.S. carriers.

Cherbo Publishing Group

Cherbo Publishing Group's business-focused, art book–quality publications, which celebrate the vital spirit of enterprise, are custom books that are used as high-impact economic development tools to enhance reputations, increase profits, and provide global exposure for businesses and organizations.

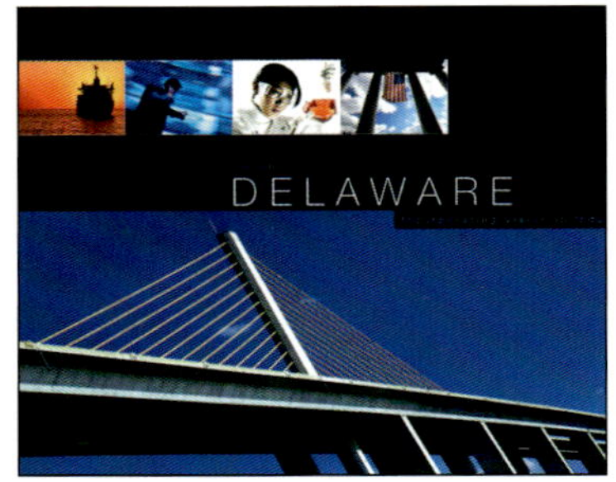

Both pages, all: Cherbo Publishing Group produces custom books for historical, professional, and government organizations. These fine publications promote the economic development of America's cities, regions, and states by chronicling their history—the people, enterprises, industries, and organizations that have made them great.

Jack Cherbo, Cherbo Publishing Group president and CEO, has been breaking new ground in the sponsored publishing business for more than 40 years.

"Previously, the cost of creating a handsome book for business developments or commemorative occasions fell directly on the sponsoring organization," Cherbo says. "My company pioneered an entirely new concept—funding these books through the sale of corporate profiles."

Cherbo honed his leading edge in Chicago, where he owned a top advertising agency before moving into publishing. Armed with a degree in business administration from Northwestern University, a mind that never stopped, and a keen sense of humor, Cherbo set out to succeed—and continues to do just that.

Cherbo Publishing Group (CPG), formerly a wholly owned subsidiary of Jostens, Inc., a Fortune 500 company, has been a privately held corporation since 1993. CPG is North America's leading publisher of quality custom books for commercial, civic, historical, and trade associations. Publications range from hardcover state, regional, and commemorative books to softcover state and regional business reports. The company is headquartered in Encino, California, and operates regional offices in Philadelphia, Minneapolis, and Houston.

About CPG Publications

CPG has created books for some of America's leading organizations, including the U.S. Chamber of Commerce, Empire State Development, California Sesquicentennial Foundation, Chicago O'Hare International Airport, and the Indiana Manufacturers Association. Participants have included ConAgra, Dow Chemical Company, Lucent Technologies, Merck & Company, and BlueCross/BlueShield.

CPG series range from history books to economic development/relocation books and from business reports to publications of special interest. The economic development series spotlights the outstanding economic and quality-of-life advantages of fast-growing cities, counties, regions, or states. The annual business reports provide an economic snapshot of individual cities, regions, or states. The commemorative series marks milestones for corporations, organizations, and professional and trade associations.

To find out how CPG can help you celebrate a special occasion, or for information on how to showcase your company or organization, contact Jack Cherbo at 818-783-0040, extension 26, or visit www.cherbopub.com.

Select CPG Publications

VISIONS OF OPPORTUNITY
City, Regional, and State Series

ALABAMA *The Progress, The Promise*

AMERICA & THE SPIRIT OF ENTERPRISE
Century of Progress, Future of Promise

CALIFORNIA *Golden Past, Shining Future*

CONNECTICUT *Chartered for Progress*

DELAWARE *Incorporating Vision in Industry*

EVANSVILLE *At the Heart of Success*

FORT WORTH *Where the Best Begins*

GREATER PHOENIX
Expanding Horizons

INDIANA
Crossroads of Industry and Innovation

LUBBOCK, TEXAS
Gem of the South Plains

MICHIGAN *America's Pacesetter*

MILWAUKEE *Midwestern Metropolis*

MISSOURI *Gateway to Enterprise*

NEW YORK STATE *Prime Mover*

NORTH CAROLINA *The State of Minds*

OKLAHOMA *The Center of It All*

SOUTH DAKOTA *Pioneering the Future*

TOLEDO *Access. Opportunity. Edge.*

UPSTATE NEW YORK
Corridor to Progress

WESTCHESTER COUNTY, NEW YORK
Headquarters to the World

WEST VIRGINIA *Reaching New Heights*

LEGACY
Commemorative Series

ALBERTA AT 100
Celebrating the Legacy

BUILD IT & THE CROWDS WILL COME
Seventy-Five Years of Public Assembly

CELEBRATE SAINT PAUL
150 Years of History

DAYTON *On the Wings of Progress*

THE EXHIBITION INDUSTRY
The Power of Commerce

IDAHO *The Heroic Journey*

MINNEAPOLIS *Currents of Change*

NEW YORK STATE ASSOCIATION OF FIRE CHIEFS
Sizing Up a Century of Service

VISIONS TAKING SHAPE
Celebrating 50 Years of the Precast/ Prestressed Concrete Industry

ANNUAL BUSINESS REPORTS

MINNESOTA REPORT *2007*

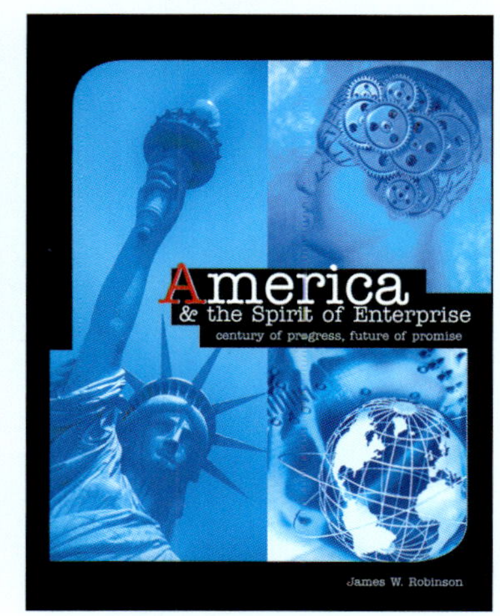

BIBLIOGRAPHY

Alegent Health. "News Center: Alegent Health Fact Sheet." http://www.alegent.com/body.cfm?id=3143 (accessed February 2006).

———. "News Center: Fact Sheets." http://www.alegent.com/body.cfm?id=2926 (accessed February 2006).

———. "News Center: Lakeside Hospital." http://www.alegent.com/body.cfm?id=2509 (accessed February 2006).

American Nurses Credentialing Center. "Magnet Facilities." http://www.nursingworld.org/ancc/magnet/facilities.html (accessed February 2006).

American Public Power Association. "Number of Public Power Utilities by State or Territory." Department of Energy, 2004. http://www.appanet.org/aboutpublic/index.cfm?ItemNumber=2691&sn.ItemNumber=2039 (accessed February 2006).

Ameritas Group. "Corporate and Group Division Overview." http://www.ameritasgroup.com/pdf/gr206.pdf (accessed March 2006).

Association of American Railroads. "Railroad Service in Nebraska 2004." December 2005. http://www.aar.org/PubCommon/Documents/AboutTheIndustry/RRState_NE.pdf?states=RRState (accessed April 2006).

———. "State Rankings." http://www.aar.org/PubCommon/Documents/AboutTheIndustry/RRState_Rankings.pdf (accessed February 2006).

Belck, Nancy, chancellor, University of Nebraska–Omaha. "Transformation: UNO's Journey to Distinction." Convocation address, October 12, 2005. http://www.unomaha.edu/chancellor/speeches/20051012_convo.php (accessed February 2006).

BryanLGH Medical Center. "BryanLGH Medical Center Orthopedics Among the Top Ten Percent in the Nation." http://www.bryanlgh.org/aboutus/news/2006/orthoHealthGrades2006.htm (accessed February 2006).

———. "BryanLGH West Phase I Expansion Opens." Press release, April 22, 2004. http://www.bryanlgh.org/aboutus/news/WestOpenhouse042204.htm (accessed February 2006).

Buffet, Warren. "Chairman's Letter." Berkshire Hathaway, December 2005. http://www.berkshirehathaway.com/letters/2005ltr.pdf (accessed February 2006).

Bureau of Business Research. "Business in Nebraska, December 2005." College of Business Administration, University of Nebraska–Lincoln. http://www.bbr.unl.edu/ (accessed February 2006).

Bureau of Labor Statistics. "Health Care and Social Assistance." http://data.bls.gov/PDQ/servlet/SurveyOutputServlet;jsessionid=f030666a363e$3F$02$3 (accessed February 2006).

Center for Rural Affairs. "Community-wide Initiatives Focused on Quality of Life Variables: Mini Homestead Acts." http://www.cfra.org/freshpromises_quality.htm (accessed March 2006).

———. "Unicameral Update." http://www.cfra.org/resources/NE_legislative_update.htm (accessed March 2006).

CNNmoney.com. "Fortune 500, 2006." http://money.cnn.com/magazines/fortune/fortune500/ (accessed March 2006).

ConAgra Foods. "Company History." http://www.conagrafoods.com/company/history/index.jsp (accessed March 2006).

———. "ConAgra Foods' The Max School Lunch Ultragrain Pizza Wins 2005 'Spirit of Innovation' Award from Prepared Foods." October 18, 2005. http://investor.conagrafoods.com/phoenix.zhtml?c=97518&p=irol-newsArticlemedia&ID=769533&highlight= (accessed March 2006).

Creighton University. "Economic Conditions." http://www.outlook-economic.com/ (accessed February 2006).

———. "University Signals that It Is 'Willing to Lead.' " http://www.creighton.edu/development/news_120305_campaign.html (accessed February 2006).

———. "Willing to Grow . . . by supporting east campus expansion." http://www.creighton.edu/development/vision_grow.html (accessed April 2006).

———. "Willing to Innovate . . . by Supporting Science Education and Technology." http://www.creighton.edu/development/vision_innovate.html (accessed February 2006).

Creighton University Medical Center. "Cancer Center—Peritoneal Neoplastic Disease." http://www.creighton.edu/CancerCenter/LoggieSpecialtyCare.html (accessed February 2006).

Creighton University School of Medicine. "Creighton M.D. Receives Prestigious Award for Bone and Mineral Research." http://medicine.creighton.edu/news/10-20-2003-ReckerAward.html (accessed February 2006).

———. "Karen Rafferty Receives National Award." http://medicine.creighton.edu/news/08-26-2005_RaffertyAward.html (accessed February 2006).

———. Office of Research. http://medicine.creighton.edu/Research/ (accessed February 2006).

Curtis-NE.com. "Roll'n Hills Addition." http://www.curtis-ne.com/rollnhillsaddition.html (accessed March 2006).

Dannebrog, Village of. "Velkommen to Dannebrog." http://www.dannebrog.org/ (accessed March 2006).

Engbretson, J. S., executive director of communications and marketing, Doane College. Telephone interview (Goodwin), February 2006.

Grand Island, City of. "Grand Island at a Glance." http://www.grand-island.com/Home/At_a_Glance/glance_index.htm (accessed March 2006).

Greater Omaha Chamber of Commerce. "Demographics." http://www.omahachamber.org/data/demographics.html (accessed March 2006).

———. "Infrastructure." http://www.accessomaha.com/MetroData/Infrastructure.asp (accessed March 2006).

Groundwater Foundation. "Fun Facts about Center Pivots." 2003 .http://www.groundwater.org/pe/rainmakers.html (accessed March 2006).

HDR. "HDR Ranked No. 1 in Healthcare Design." http://www.hdrinc.com/8/34/default.aspx?entry=279 (accessed March 2006).

———. "History." http://www.hdrinc.com/3/12/2/default.aspx (accessed March 2006).

Hovey, Art. "Switch turned on for switchgrass energy potential." *Lincoln Journal Star*, March 15, 2006. http://www.journalstar.com/articles/2006/03/15/local/doc441757ce50b1b105411252.txt (accessed March 2006).

Jenkins, Nate. "Nebraska's online usage rising." *Lincoln Journal Star*, December 10, 2005. http://www.journalstar.com/articles/2005/12/10/nebraska/doc439b60810ab33180472634.txt (accessed March 2006).

JournalStar.com. "Farmers, ranchers hunting for off-season profits." *Lincoln Journal Star*, October 22, 2005. http://www.journalstar.com/articles/2005/10/22/nebraska/doc435abda10dfa2504451602.txt (accessed March 2006).

BIBLIOGRAPHY

———. "Meeting scheduled to boost Nebraska's agricultural, ecological tourism." Associated Press, October 4, 2005. http://www.journalstar.com /articles/2005/10/04/nebraska/doc4342e96d8c41f658361246.txt (accessed March 2006).

Kearney Hub. "Web site to be one-stop shop for agritourism." *Lincoln Journal Star,* March 5, 2006. http://www.journalstar.com/articles/2006/03/05 /nebraska/doc440b66b59cb61951998018.txt (accessed March 2006).

Knoll, Robert E. *Prairie University: A History of the University of Nebraska.* Lincoln: University of Nebraska Press, 1995.

Kooser, Ted. *Delights & Shadows.* Port Townsend, Wash.: Copper Canyon Press, 2004.

Larsen, Lawrence H., and Barbara J. Cottrell. *The Gate City: A History of Omaha.* Lincoln: University of Nebraska Press, 1997.

Lincoln Convention and Visitors Bureau. "Facts & Figures." http://www.lincoln .org/visiting/facts.htm (accessed March 2006).

Lonsdale, Richard E., ed. *Economic Atlas of Nebraska.* Lincoln: University of Nebraska Press, 1977.

MBA Poultry. "Initial Processing to Continue in Tecumseh." March 4, 2005. http://www.smartchicken.com/wisc.html (accessed March 2006).

Modernhealthcare.com. "Solucient's 100 Top Hospitals." Crain Communications. http://www.modernhealthcare.com/page.cms?pageId=757&potId=100 (accessed February 2006).

Modern Woodmen of the World. "History." http://www.woodmen.com/ inside.cfm?Main_menu_id=1&Sub_menu_id=3&Page_id=126 (accessed March 2006).

Morgan Quitno Press. "Results of the 2005 Healthiest State Award: Which State Is Healthiest?" http://www.morganquitno.com/hcrank05.htm (accessed March 2006).

———. "Results of the 2005 Most Livable State Award: Which State Is the Most Livable?" http://www.morganquitno.com/sr05mlrnk.htm (accessed March 2006).

———. "Results of the 2005 Smartest State Award: Which State Is Smartest?" http://www.morganquitno.com/edrank.htm (accessed March 2006).

Mutual of Omaha. "About Mutual of Omaha's Wild Kingdom." http://www .wildkingdom.com/about/ (accessed April 2006).

———. "2005 Annual Report." http://www.mutualofomaha.com/acrodocs /about/annual_report.pdf (accessed March 2006).

Nebraska Advantage. "Training Nebraska's workforce gets full support." http://www.nebraskaadvantage.biz/pr9.htm (accessed March 2006).

Nebraska Agricultural Statistics Service. "Nebraska Agriculture Fact Card." February 2006. http://www.agr.state.ne.us/facts.pdf (accessed March 2006).

Nebraska Agriculture Industry Partnership. "The Numbers." http://www .nebraskalivestock.org/industry/facts_figures.cfm (accessed March 2006).

Nebraska Center for Entrepreneurship. "Overview of the Center." College of Business Administration, University of Nebraska–Lincoln. http://www .cba.unl.edu/outreach/ent/about.html (accessed February 2006).

Nebraska Community College System. "Business and Industry Training Guide." Undated pamphlet.

Nebraska Corn Board. "NE Corn Facts: Corn Utilization." Nebraska Department of Agriculture. http://www.nebraskacorn.org/necornfacts/cornutilization.htm (accessed March 2006).

———. "NE Corn Facts: Irrigation." Nebraska Department of Agriculture. http://www.nebraskacorn.org/necornfacts/irrigation.htm (accessed March 2006).

Nebraska Department of Agriculture. "Beginning Farmer." http://www.agr.state.ne.us/division/med/begfrm.htm (accessed March 2006).

Nebraska Department of Economic Development. "AAA Ranks Nebraska #1." Press release, March 24, 2005. http://pio.neded.org/press/2005/05rel21.htm (accessed March 2006).

———. "Business Climate: USA Heartland Market." (See also pdf link to "Discover the Possibilities" pamphlet.) http://business.neded.org/businessclimate.htm (accessed March 2006).

———. "Census of Agriculture 2004: Number and Average Acres of Nebraska Farms and Ranches." U.S. Department of Agriculture. http://info.neded.org/stathand/esecc1.gif (accessed March 2006).

———. "Manufacturers Arranged by Product Category January 2004." http://www.neded.org/2004mfgproduct.pdf (accessed March 2006).

———. "Nebraska Advantage Incentives Overview." http://www.nebraskaadvantage.biz/overview.htm (accessed March 2006).

———. "Nebraska Annual Economic Performance Indicators." October 2005. http://info.neded.org/econperf/bnchmrk2.htm (accessed March 2006).

———. "Nebraska's courses rank in top 20." Press release, September 16, 2004. http://pio.neded.org/press/2004/04rel113.htm (accessed March 2006).

———. "Nebraska's History." http://info.neded.org/stathand/parttwo/nehist5y.html (accessed March 2006).

———. "Nebraska Travel and Tourism Facts." http://info.neded.org/tourfact.htm (accessed March 2006).

———. "Nebraska Urban and Rural Populations." http://info.neded.org/stathand/bsecc2.gif (accessed March 2006).

———. "Number and Employment of Construction Establishments with Payroll." http://info.neded.org/stathand/isecc6.gif (accessed March 2006).

Nebraska Department of Education. "86 Percent of Nebraska 4th, 8th, 11th Graders Proficient on State Writing Assessment." Press release, August 25, 2005. http://www.nde.state.ne.us/ndepress/2005/082505.htm (accessed March 2006).

———. "Nebraska's Average ACT Score Higher, Continues to Outpace National Average." Press release, August 17, 2005. http://www.nde.state.ne.us/ndepress/2005/08172005.htm (accessed March 2006).

Nebraska Department of Roads. "Current Needs Assessment 2005" and "Programming New Construction Projects." http://www.nebraskatransportation.org/projects/ (accessed February 2006).

———. "Fact Sheet: The Interstate in Nebraska." http://www.dor.state.ne.us/i-80-anniv/index.htm (accessed February 2006).

———. "Nebraska Long-Range Transportation Plan: Summary of Existing and Future Conditions and Transportation System." 2005. http://www.nebraskatransportation.org/lrtp/ (accessed February 2006).

Nebraska Division of Travel and Tourism. "Nebraska's Scenic Byways." http://www.visitnebraska.org/byways/index.htm (accessed March 2006).

BIBLIOGRAPHY

———. "Nebraska Trivia." http://www.visitnebraska.org/pressroom/facts/trivia.htm (accessed March 2006).

Nebraska Dry Bean Commission. "Nebraska Quality Grown Dry Edible Beans." http://www.nebraskadrybean.com/beans.htm (accessed March 2006).

Nebraska Energy Office. "Ethanol Production by State." http://www.neo.ne.gov/statshtml/121.htm (accessed May 2006).

Nebraska.gov. "Nebraska Colleges & Universities." http://www.nebraska.gov/portal.php?section=education&lvl1=211&lvl2=0&lvl3=0&lvl4=0&lvl5=0&lvl6=0&lvl7=0&lvl8=0&lvl9=0 (accessed April 2006).

Nebraska Grain Sorghum Producers Association. "Tell Me About Grain Sorghum . . ." http://www.nesorghum.com/linksfromhomepage/tellmefromhomepage/tellmeinfofromhomelink.htm (accessed March 2006).

Nebraska Medical Center. "About the Nebraska Medical Center." http://www.nebraskamed.com/media_center/about.shtml (accessed February 2006).

———. "J.D. Power and Associates Reports: The Nebraska Medical Center Recognized for Providing an Outstanding Patient Experience." Press release, October 17, 2005. http://www.nebraskamed.com/index.htm (accessed February 2006).

———. "The Nebraska Medical Center Organ Transplant Program." http://www.nebraskamed.com/transplant/ (accessed February 2006).

Nebraska Policy Institute. "Completed Research: Economic Importance of Irrigated Agriculture 2003." http://www.nebraskapolicy.org/ (accessed March 2006).

Nebraska Pork Producers Association. "October Is National Pork Month." http://www.nepork.org/5news/news.php?newsitem=2005092013 (accessed March 2006).

Nebraska Public Power District. Brewster, Nebraska. "Spirit of the Cowboy." http://www.ci.brewster.ne.us/ (accessed March 2006).

———. Wilbur, Nebraska. "Vitáme Vás: We Welcome You." http://www.ci.wilber.ne.us/ (accessed March 2006).

Nebraska Public Service Commission. "2005 Annual Report on Telecommunications." http://www.psc.state.ne.us/home/NPSC/communication/AnnualReport2005.pdf (accessed March 2006).

Nebraska's Coordinating Commission for Postsecondary Education. "2005 Nebraska Higher Education Progress Report for the LR75 Legislative Evaluation Task Force: Volume One." http://www.ccpe.state.ne.us/publicdoc/ccpe/Reports/LR174/2005/default.asp (accessed February 2006).

Nebraska State College System. "Governor Heineman Issues Proclamation Declaring Nebraska State College System Month in October." http://www.nscs.edu/release/State%20College%20Month.htm (accessed February 2006).

Nebraska Unicameral Legislature. *Nebraska Blue Book* online, 2004–05 edition. http://www.unicam.state.ne.us/bluebook/intro/economy/pdf (accessed March 2006).

Nebraska Wesleyan University. "Watson to Retire as President of Nebraska Wesleyan University." Press release, February 3, 2006. http://www.nebrwesleyan.edu/media/news.php (accessed February 2006).

Nebraska Workforce Development. "2002 to 2012 Long-term Industry Employment Projections: Statewide—Nebraska." Nebraska Department of Labor, September 2004. http://www.dol.state.ne.us/nwd/workserv/jobcareer/proj/nebraska.htm (accessed February and April 2006).

Nelnet. "Corporate." http://www.nelnet.net/corporate.asp (accessed March 2006).

Nelson, Chris Christen. "Metro Guide 2005: Piecing together the Omaha–Council Bluffs metro area." *Omaha World-Herald*, August 7, 2005.

O'Connor, Tom, UNMC Public Affairs. E-mail interview (Goodwin), February 2006.

O'Hanlon, Kevin. "Displaced Tyson Workers Transfer to Plants." Associated Press story on Forbes.com, March 15, 2006. http://www.forbes.com/feeds/ap/2006/03/15/ap2597881.html (accessed April 2006).

Olson, James C., and Ronald C. Naugle. *History of Nebraska*. Lincoln: University of Nebraska Press, 1997.

Olsson Associates. "About—History." http://www.oaconsulting.com/about_history.htm (accessed March 2006).

———. "News & Events—Facts About OA." http://www.oaconsulting.com/news_facts.htm (accessed March 2006).

———. "News & Events—Rankings & Awards." http://www.oaconsulting.com/news_awards.htm (accessed March 2006).

———. "Projects: Antelope Valley." http://www.oaconsulting.com/project_indi.asp?ID=120 (accessed March 2006).

O'Neill, City of. "City of O'Neill Welcomes You to Nebraska's Irish Capital." http://www.cityofoneill.com/ (accessed March 2006).

Pearson, Melinda, AIA, executive director, Nebraska Board of Engineers and Architects. E-mail interview (Goodwin).

Perlman, Harvey. "State of the University Address, 2005." Speech, University of Nebraska–Lincoln, September 9, 2005. http://www.unl.edu/pr/chancllr/sua2005/ (accessed February 2006).

Peru State College. "Peru State Listed Fourth in the Nation for College 'Best Buy.' " Press release. http://marketing.peru.edu/geteducated.htm (accessed February 2006).

Phaidon Press. "Phaidon Atlas of Contemporary World Architecture." Press release. http://www.phaidon.com/atlas/phaidon_press_release.pdf (accessed March 2006).

Piersol, Richard. "Molex hums along quietly at the top of its industry." *Lincoln Journal Star*, February 19, 2006. http://www.journalstar.com/articles/2006/02/25/business/doc43ff91bd4dff5507631108.txt (accessed March 2006).

———. "Molex sold on Kearney grads." *Lincoln Journal Star*, February 25, 2006. http://www.journalstar.com/articles/2006/02/25/business/doc43ff941a25cc9852269077.txt (accessed February and April 2006).

Princeton Review. "Creighton University." http://www.princetonreview.com/college/research/profiles/schoolsays.asp?category=1&listing=1023809&LTID=1&intbucketid= (accessed February 2006).

Randy Brown Architects. "Firm Info: Awards." www.randybrownarchitects.com (accessed March 2006).

St. Elizabeth Regional Medical Center. "Burn and Wound Care Center." http://www.saintelizabethonline.com/index.php?lev=81&page_id=81&pp=68 (accessed February 2006).

———. "Lincoln's Oldest Hospital." http://www.saintelizabethonline.com/index.php?lev=289&page_id=316&pp=71 (accessed February 2006).

SHG Resources. "Nebraska Timeline of State History." SHG, 2003. http://www.shgresources.com/ne/timeline/ (accessed April 2006).

Sitel. "Fact Sheet." http://www.sitel.com/Content.asp?id=140 (accessed March 2006).

BIBLIOGRAPHY

Tyson Foods. "Plant Consolidation to Increase Efficiency: Strategy involves closing two Nebraska plants." February 15, 2006. http://www.tysonfoodsinc.com /PressRoom/ViewArticle.aspx?id=2102 (accessed March 2006).

UNIFI Companies. "Historical Snapshots." http://www.unificompanies.com /unifi_423.htm (accessed March 2006).

Union Pacific Corporation. "Bailey Yard." http://www.uprr.com/aboutup /history/bailey/index (accessed February 2006).

———. "Company Overview." http://www.uprr.com/aboutup/uprrover.shtml (accessed February 2006).

United Health Foundation. "America's Health Rankings 2005 Edition." http://www.unitedhealthfoundation.org/shr2005/states/Nebraska.html (accessed March 2006).

United States Strategic Command. "U.S. Strategic Command History." http://www.stratcom.mil/about-ch.html (accessed March 2006).

University of Nebraska. "History." University of Nebraska Board of Regents. http://www.nebraska.edu/about/about_history.shtml (accessed February 2006).

University of Nebraska–Kearney. "Industrial Distribution Program." Industrial Distribution Organization. http://www.unkid.org/degree_req.html (accessed April 2006).

———. "UNK: A Quick Overview." http://www.unk.edu/about/fastfacts /index.php?id=100 (accessed February 2006).

University of Nebraska–Lincoln. "Business in Nebraska, December 2005." Bureau of Business Research, Nebraska College of Business Administration. http://www.bbr.unl.edu/ (accessed February 2006).

———. "Nebraska Newspapers: A Brief History." UNL Libraries. http://www.unl.edu/nebnews/newshis.html (accessed April 2006).

———. "Nebraska Positioned to Be a Leader in the Expanding Biofuels Industry." Institute of Agriculture and Natural Resources, July 21, 2005. http://ianrnews.unl.edu/static/0507210.shtml (accessed February 2006).

———. "New Internship Program Focuses on Technology in Rural Development." J. D. Edwards Honors Program, June 12, 2003. http://jdedwards .unl.edu/press/print_release.asp?prid=9 (accessed February 2006).

University of Nebraska Medical Center. "Board of Regents approve completion of construction of Center for Health Sciences Education at UNMC." Press release, January 20, 2006. http://app1.unmc.edu/publicaffairs/newsarchive /view_art.cfm?article_id=1252 (accessed February 2006).

———. "History of UNMC." http://www.unmc.edu/5/aboutunmc/history.htm (accessed February 2006).

———. "Rural Health Education Network & Nebraska Area Health Education Centers." http://www.unmc.edu/dept/rhen/ (accessed February 2006).

———. "UNMC exceeds goals for research funding." http://www.unmc.edu/5 /research/research.htm (accessed February 2006).

University of Nebraska State Museum and Nebraska Game and Parks Commission. "Paleontological Finds 1991–2000." Ashfall Fossil Beds State Historical Park. http://ashfall.unl.edu/paleofinds.html (accessed March 2006).

University of Nebraska Technology Park. "Park Resources." http://www .unebtechpark.com/Park_Resources.asp (accessed February 2006).

U.S. Department of Agriculture. "Number, Land Area, Average Size, and Value of Farms: Nebraska—Selected Years." National Agricultural Statistics Service, Census of Agriculture, 2004. http://info.neded.org/stathand/esect1.htm (accessed March 2006).

U.S. Department of Commerce. "Summary of Selected Housing Characteristics: Nebraska—Census Years 1960 to 2000 and 2003." Bureau of the Census. http://info.neded.org/stathand/isect6.htm (accessed March 2006).

———. "Summary Statistics by 2002 NAICS: Nebraska." Economic census of 2002. http://www.census.gov/econ/census02/data/ne/NE000.HTM (accessed March 2006).

U.S. Department of Energy. "Average Price of Natural Gas Delivered to Residential Consumers by State, 2004." Energy Information Administration. http://www.eia.doe.gov/neic/rankings/gasresprice.htm (accessed February 2006).

U.S. News & World Report. "America's Best Colleges 2006: Midwestern Universities—Master's: Top Schools." http://www.usnews.com/usnews/edu/college/rankings/brief/univmas/ummidwest/tier1/t1univmas_mw_brief.php (accessed February 2006).

U.S. Poultry and Egg Association. "U.S. Egg Industry Fact Sheet—April 2006." http://www.poultryegg.org/EconomicInfo/docs/EggFactSheet.pdf (accessed April 2006).

Water Center, Institute of Agriculture and Natural Resources. "Water FAQs: Nebraska Water Fun Facts." University of Nebraska–Lincoln. http://watercenter.unl.edu/water_information/nebraska_water.htm (accessed March 2006).

Western Sugar Cooperative. "About Us." http://www.westernsugar.com/about_today.asp (accessed March 2006).

The Web sites of the following companies and organizations were consulted as well:

Answers.com; Boys Town National Research Hospital; Center for Afghanistan Studies, University of Nebraska–Omaha; Chief Buildings; Chief Industries; City of Bellevue, Nebraska; Crete Carrier Corporation; Nebraska Cattlemen; Nebraska Ethanol Board; Nebraska Logistics Council; Nebraska Public Power District; Nebraska State Historical Society; Nebraska Trucking Association; Nebraska Water Policy Task Force; NU Skills; Pharma-Chemie; Streck Laboratories; U.S. Department of Commerce; Valmont Industries; and Werner Enterprises.

INDEX

D

E

F

INDEX

INDEX

INDEX

PHOTO CREDITS

Page ii: © Chad Bell
Page v: Courtesy, Nebraska Division of Travel and Tourism. Photo by J. Nabb
Page vi, center: © Richard Cummins
Page vi, left: © Keith Ghormley
Pages vi–vii: © Steve Sprengel
Page viii, left: © Jim Richardson/Corbis
Page viii, right: © Katherin Malagón
Page ix: © Wade Fruhling
Page xi: © Orjan F. Ellingvag/Corbis
Page xiii: © Lise Gagne
Page xv: © Masterfile
Page xvi: Courtesy G. Ryan, Nebraska DED
Page xvii, left: Courtesy M. Forsberg, Nebraska DED
Page xvii, right: Courtesy M. Forsberg, Nebraska DED
Page xviii, left: © Corbis
Page xviii, right: © Kevin Dodge/Masterfile
Page 1: Courtesy, University of Nebraska at Kearney
Page 2, left: Courtesy, Mid-Manhattan Library/Picture Collection
Page 2, top right: Courtesy, Library of Congress
Page 2, bottom right: © Getty Images
Pages 2–3, background: Courtesy, New York Public Library/Humanities and Social Sciences Library/The Lionel Pincus and Princess Firyal Map Division
Page 3, left: Courtesy, Library of Congress
Page 3, right: © Bettmann/CORBIS
Page 4, top left: Courtesy, Library of Congress
Page 4, bottom left: Courtesy, Library of Congress
Page 4, right: © Michael Ochs Archives/Corbis
Page 5, top: © Bettmann/CORBIS
Page 5, right: © Time Life Pictures/ Getty Images
Page 5, bottom left: Courtesy, Library of Congress
Page 6, left: © Corbis
Page 6, right: © Bettmann/CORBIS
Page 7, top left: © Bettmann/CORBIS
Page 7, right: © G.E. Kidder Smith/CORBIS
Page 7, bottom left: © Michael Ochs Archives/Corbis
Page 8, left: © Wally McNamee/ CORBIS
Page 8, top right: © Cynthia Johnson/ Time Life Pictures/Getty Image
Page 8, bottom right: © The Bettmann Archive/Corbis

PHOTO CREDITS

Page 9, top left: © Nancy R. Schiff/ Hulton Archive/Getty Images
Page 9, right: © Donald Miralle/ Getty Images
Page 9, center: © Michael Kim/Corbis
Page 10: © David Cannon/Getty Image
Page 12: © Joel Sartore/National Geographic Image Collection
Page 13: Courtesy, HDR. Photography by Tom Kessler.
Page 14: © Painet
Page 15, top: © Lorenz Britt/Alamy
Page 15, bottom: © Roy Ooms
Page 16, left: © James L. Amos/Corbis
Page 16, right: © Phil Schermeister/CORBIS
Page 17: © M. Forsberg, Nebraska DED
Page 18: © Richard Cummins
Page 19: © Alan R. Moller/Getty Images
Page 20: © Icon SMI/Corbis
Page 21: © Jean-Erick Pasquier/ Rapho/Imagestate
Pages 22–23: © Joseph Giitter
Page 23, bottom: © James Colburn
Page 23, top: Courtesy, Nebraska Division of Travel and Tourism. Photo by Erik Stenbakken.
Page 24: Courtesy, Nebraska Division of Travel and Tourism. Photo by Erik Stenbakken.
Page 25: © M. Forsberg, Nebraska DED
Page 26: © Mitch Kezar/Getty Images
Page 27, bottom: © Amanda Rohde
Page 27, top: © Darin Epperly/Getty Images
Page 28: © Stock Image/Pixland/Alamy
Page 29, bottom: © Tom Stewart/ Corbis
Page 29, top: © SGO/Image Point FR/Corbis
Page 30: © Ronnie Kaufman/Corbis
Page 32: © Corbis
Page 33, bottom spot: © Michael Westhoff
Page 33, top: © Gary Moon/age foto-stock
Page 33, top spot: © AGStockUSA, Inc./Alamy
Page 34, spot: © Macduff Everton/Corbis
Pages 34–35: © Gary Moon/age foto-stock
Page 35, center: © Valerie Simmons/Masterfile
Page 35, right: © David Zanzinger
Page 36–37: © Jim Wark/Index Stock Imagery
Page 37, right: © Don Klumpp/The Image Bank/Getty Images
Page 38, left: © Getty Images
Page 39: © David R. Frazier Photolibrary, Inc./Alamy

Page 40: © Macduff Everton/Corbis

Page 41, left: © Philip & Karen Smith/age fotostock

Page 41, right: Courtesy M. Forsberg, Nebraska DED

Page 42: © Don Solotorovsky

Page 43, left: © Andre Jenny

Page 43, right: © Richard Cummins

Page 44: © Mario Tama/Getty Images

Page 45: Courtesy, Nelnet

Page 46: © Bill Varie/Corbis

Page 47: © Tim Pannell/Corbis

Page 48: © Photodisc

Page 49: © Zubin Shroff/Getty Images

Page 50: © Corbis

Page 51: Courtesy, HDR. Photography by Tom Kessler.

Page 52: © Mika/zefa/Corbis

Page 53: © Edward Pond/Masterfile

Page 54, left: Courtesy, University of Nebraska-Lincoln Extension

Page 54, right: Courtesy, University of Nebraska Technology Park

Page 55: © Benjamin J. Smith

Pages 56–57: © Steve Sprengel

Page 58, center: Courtesy, University of Nebraska Medical Center. Photo by Ryan Cole.

Page 58, left: Courtesy, University of Nebraska Medical Center

Page 58, right: Courtesy, University of Nebraska Medical Center

Page 59: Courtesy, University of Nebraska Medical Center

Pages 60–61: Photo by Jed Godsey, Parachute College Program, Parachute, Inc.

Page 61, right: © Tom Stewart/Corbis

Page 62: © Jon Feingersh/Masterfile

Page 63: © Masterfile

Page 64, left: © Corbis

Page 64, right: Courtesy, Boys Town National Research Hospital

Page 65: © Digital Vision

Pages 66–67: Courtesy, University of Nebraska Medical Center

Page 68: Courtesy, Alegent

Page 69: Courtesy, Alegent

Page 70: © Getty Images

Page 71, left: © Peter M. Fisher/Corbis

Page 71, right: © Mario Villafuerte/Getty Images

Page 72: © Owaki–Kulla/Corbis

Page 73: © Ramin Talaie/Corbis

Page 74: Courtesy, Greater Omaha Steaks

Page 75: © David Zanzinger

Page 76: © Volkmar Wentzel/Getty Images

Page 77: © Tim Macpherson/Getty Images

PHOTO CREDITS

Page 78, left: © Elliott Kaufman/Beateworks/Corbis
Page 78, right: © pixonaut
Page 79: © Jeff Hochstrasse
Page 80: Courtesy, Molex Connector Corporation
Page 81: Photo Provided by Chief Agri Industrial Division
Page 82: © Comstock Images/Alamy
Page 83: © Philip Gould/Corbis
Page 84, left: © Macduff Everton/Corbis
Page 84, right: © David R. Frazier Photolibrary, Inc./Alamy
Page 85: © Mike Malone/Malone and Company Photography
Pages 86–87: © Jeff Epler
Page 88, bottom left: © Frederick Gay
Page 88, right: © Andre Jenny/Alamy
Page 88, top left: © David Gilmore
Page 89, left: Courtesy, Nebraska Division of Travel and Tourism. Photo by J. Nabb.
Page 89, right: Courtesy, NEBRASKAland Magazine/Nebraska Game and Parks Commission
Page 90: Courtesy, Nebraska Public Power District
Page 91, bottom: Courtesy, Nebraska Public Power District
Page 91, top: © Superstock
Page 92: © Photodisc
Page 94: © Richard Cummins
Page 97: © Richard Cummins/SuperStock
Page 98: © Rob Melnychuk/Getty images
Page 103: © Joey Nigh/Corbis
Page 104: © James McQuillan
Page 111: © Corbis
Page 112: © Tim Pohl
Page 119: © TexPhoto
Page 120: © José Luis Gutiérrez
Page 135: © BJ Formento/age fotostock
Page 136: © Corbis
Page 154: © Corbis
Page 159: © Roberto Adrian
Page 160: © Alvaro Heinzen
Page 168: © Tomas Kraus
Page 175: © Superstock
Page 176: © Richard Gerstner
Page 181: © Richard Cummins
Page 184: © Corbis
Page 189: © Jennifer Trenchard
Page 190: © Eric Audras/age fotostock
Page 193: © Eva Serrabassa
Page 195: © Chris Machian/Prairie Pixel Group
Page 196: © Bernd Klumpp
Page 199: © Photodisc

cherbo publishing group, inc.

TYPOGRAPHY

Principal faces used: Adobe Garamond, designed by Robert Slimbach in 1989, which was derived from previous designs by Claude Garamond, Jean Jannon, and Robert Granjon; Neue Helvetica, designed by Edouard Hoffmann and Max Miedinger in 1983

HARDWARE

Macintosh G5 desktops, digital color laser printing with Xerox Docucolor 12, digital imaging with Creo EverSmart Supreme

SOFTWARE

QuarkXPress, Adobe Illustrator, Adobe Photoshop, Adobe Acrobat, Microsoft Word, Eye-One Pro by Gretagmacbeth, Creo Oxygen, FlightCheck

PAPER

Text Paper: #80 Luna Matte

Bound in Rainbow® recycled content papers from Ecological Fibers, Inc.

Dust Jacket: #100 Sterling-Litho Gloss

NEBRASKA

CENTERED ON THE LAND